STOP GETTING FU*KED BY TECHNICAL RECRUITERS

A NERD'S GUIDE TO NEGOTIATING SALARY AND BENEFITS

SCOTT TURMAN

BRIGHTRAY PUBLISHING

DEDICATION

This book is dedicated to its very enemy, because there do exist a few technical recruiters that helped me get into some organizations that most developers can only dream of. While I am clearly critical of many of your methods, misdirections, and lack of actual IT knowledge, I will always be in awe of your ability to sell something that you know so little about. You're not all bad, but the bad ones really bring down the entire profession.

To my beautiful wife:
    You are my life and my love. There is no me without you, and I love you with all of my heart.

To my amazing son:
    If it wasn't for you, this book would have been done a full year earlier. ;) I love you.

To my father and David Christensen:
    You know you're drunk when you hit a coastguard station.

FOREWORD

Don't skip this part. I know you're in a hurry, but this is critical.

Friends,

I'm in a bit of a paradox: I have an exceedingly low opinion for almost all so-called "technical" recruiters while also owing a great deal of my career to their sales skills. Without them, I probably wouldn't have had a shot in Hell at the dream organizations that they were able to get me into. I count NASA and Disney as just a few of those. Technical recruiters have opened doors where I had only seen walls, and yet I'll be the first to call them snakes.

I understand, maybe even better than most, the value in identifying capable people. Linking good people to good jobs, that's important. But in the world of recruiting for IT technology, it's somehow become all sales and no technology. We have a saying for that in Texas: "it's all cowboy hats and no cattle". We're being sold by people who don't even know the industry that they exploit.

Over the past few years, I've seen recruiters charging

higher and higher rates, but I haven't seen this translate back to the rates paid to the people doing the actual work. How many of you have been mistakenly forwarded an email that gave away what the recruiter was getting for you? I bet you were surprised.

This book is going to show you how to take the power back. You are the prize and negotiating for a higher rate is more than within your reach. You are the one with the skills needed to make technology go, and a recruiting company is simply one of many conduits to get to the work that's out there in the world.

I first realized how negotiable this delta between what they were paying me and what they were charging for me was while I had been working a contract at the Golf Channel (which, as a side note, is really a wonderful place to work [and in the interest of full disclosure, my wife currently works for NBC Universal which, at the time of this book, owns the Golf Channel]).

The staffing company had a rule that prohibited consultants to disclose what they were making. I'm pretty sure that this has since been made illegal. At the time, though, I had to sign a contract that effectively kept my mouth shut about my own money. This was when I really started to question, for the first time ever, what it was that they were charging for me.

My rate there was $38 an hour. A manager eventually admitted to me that they were paying over $90/h for me. Quick math: that's a difference of $52/hour that I wasn't making, which meant the staffing company was making $108k a year on me. If I had had that kind of information before signing the contract and knew what I was doing, I could have easily negotiated for a much higher rate. I mean, they were making more per hour doing *nothing* than I actually was while working. I don't even need to tell you how outrageous that is. I, of course, was a bit outraged.

But this experience shook me to see just how much sky really exists in this game. FYI, salary negotiation is a game, and you're going to have to start thinking that. And you'll have to stop taking this process so personally, too.

That weird, tight feeling you get in your chest when you tell your adversary your number? It's a differing mix of guilt, shame, and excitement. You're going to learn how to stop letting these emotions cloud your state of mind during these critical sit-downs. How nervous do you think the recruiter/trained negotiator is? I can promise you that their heart rate stays stock-steady, because they do this shit about twenty times a week. Your ability in negotiating might mean the difference between a comfortable living or just barely paying your bills; this is just their job. And they get to hone their skill every day, whereas you probably won't get to practice this more than ten times in your entire career. This is obviously anything but a fair fight.

But we're going to even it out a little. Learning how to negotiate for a better rate may be one of the most important life skills that you can ever develop. This book is a collection of what I've learned in my many-year career, and how to accomplish this. It is my hope that you'll see the value of this book when you stop and realize that for every, say, $10 extra hourly that you're able to squeeze from a recruiter/employer, you're going to get another $20k-ish more per year. That's no chump change that you're trying to haggle over, that's a *living*. It's also important to consider that every salary also has an additive effect over the lifetime of your total earnings.

You don't have to work for less than you're worth. In fact, it's your personal duty not to. Allow me to remind you that the lifespan of the average human is about 70 years. If you're seeing this in your twenties, you've got some time. If you're in your forties, though, then you really should consider that there is a pretty good chance that you'll be dead in the next 30 years.

Tick-tock. It's already later than you think.

Your Friend,

Scott

To the Recruiters,

I've been accused of biting the hand that has fed my family and me for over 25 years. The derogatory and insulting parts of this book are not, of course, aimed at all recruiters. The derogatory and insulting parts of this book are for the second-rate-used-car-salesmen-type recruiters that are destroying an industry that they neither invented or innovated. I hope this book makes your life harder.

Kisses,

Scott

INTRODUCTION

I started my career buying into the same bullshit given to all potential hires:

"We don't pay more than x percentage of your most recent position because that's just not how things work."

It doesn't take that much experience to recognize this as complete and total bullshit. Any recent graduate of a university, middle school, or clown college can see that that statement doesn't really make sense. But they still may accept it at face value because, hey, it's not easy to outright challenge the supposed system in place.

Recruiters are aware of this, and that's what they prey on. This is known as setting a base in negotiations. They feed you this lie so that they can lower your base number. The lower they can start you, obviously, means the lower that they can ultimately get you for.

But here's the thing: if you are able to provide a needed service or skill set, then you should be able to ask for a rate that is commensurable to the gig. Period.

Technology is unlike most other job markets. If there are

only thirty-five candidates in the entire state that have the skills or technology stack needed, then you'd better negotiate accordingly. A real (or simply perceived) scarcity in the type of candidate required will help you win the salary that you're looking for.

For example, my organization had once been trying to hire for an EDI technology called Sterling Integrator. We'd been looking for over five months. Do a quick search on LinkedIn and you'll see that there exist less than 2,200 people in the entire United States that have any experience with this stack. And exactly how many out of those 2,200 do you think would be willing to relocate for this gig? 100? 50? Half of zero? This rare kind of person is known as a Unicorn for a reason. And I'm not sure if I've ever interviewed a candidate that had understood this.

One of these Unicorns reached out to us, completely out of the blue. We normally try to get an understanding of their rates early on in the process, so nobody's time gets wasted if we can't afford them. Well this Unicorn, we'll call him Carl, he was a little green. He'd had maybe four years of experience in this stack, probably even less. When I asked him what he was currently making, I was really only trying to peg him to a low starting point. Carl told me that he was making about sixty grand a year, which was ridiculously low for his skill set. Remember, this was our Unicorn, our one out of twenty-two hundred. How much do you think we would be willing to pay for him, would we be *happy* to pay to snag him?

So knowing his current salary, I asked him what he was looking for to take this position. What could we get our Unicorn for? Carl parroted back the exact same bullshit I've heard from every recruiter and HR rep through my entire career:

"Well, I'm making sixty-thousand now, so I would be very

happy with a twenty-percent raise." So, that was our Unicorn. In his own words, *happy* to hand himself over for the low low price of 72k.

If he'd done any research or had even just spoken to some of his peers, Carl would have known that he was probably worth over double his salary (don't get out your calculator, that figures out to over 120k a year). And if he knew how to really dazzle his client, he could have gotten even more. Yet there he was, offering himself for the near criminal underselling of seventy-two thousand.

But he must have also realized that the rate range the company had given me was already set in stone. I later learned that he actually did know what he was worth, but he just didn't have neither the skill or the guts to ask for it. And this is the exact issue for 90% of the technology workers out there.

Not asking for what you're worth is the absolute best way to not get it. Playing by some lame set of rules cooked up thirty years ago by an HR manager or used-car salesman is just dumb. What you have to understand is that you start negotiations the very moment that you first make contact with an organization. Most people don't see that the negotiations table is only the very end of the process, not the start.

You have to be primed for battle right when you answer the initial phone call. You have to be ready to make your case for a high(er) salary. You need to know how you'll respond to the trap of: "How much are you looking for?" And you'll have to resist the impulse to tell them what you currently make, as this will always end up as their basis for your new salary.

As an aside, I ended up offering Carl 110k and lowered my cut from the client because I both have a soul and would like to retain the ability to sleep at night. The way I saw it, a higher rate would keep Carl from being poached by the next guy, so it worked out best for everyone involved. I also sat him down and taught him how to negotiate like I would with anyone who has ever worked for me.

You don't work for me. We don't even know each other, and probably never will. But since you've decided to invest the money and time to read this, I'll teach you everything that I've learned out there.

CHAPTER ONE: THE GAME

TLDR (for the fellow elderly, this stands for "too long, didn't read", or a short summary of what this chapter covers):

- Technical recruiters are the inevitable block between us and employment.
- Technical recruiters do not understand our industry. Their objective is to push us into jobs as quickly as possible and at the lowest rate that they can get us for.
- Not every call is really going to be about a job opportunity. Recruiters can and will contact you in an attempt to get information about something else.
- Do not ever tell a recruiter anything that doesn't ultimately benefit you. No question they ask is ever innocent. You are always free to refuse an answer.
- Salary negotiation is a game that you can't get emotional about. You have to approach this as

objectively as the trained opponent that you're going against.

- You are ultimately responsible for getting what you need. If you want to get what you're worth, you have to ask for it.

UNDERSTANDING YOUR ADVERSARY

I've been working as a moderately-priced technology prostitute for over twenty-five years now: writing code for the likes of NASA, a couple DOD contracts, working for the Florida House of Representatives, Hilton, Disney, as well as a cavalcade of couple-month gigs at other organizations not worth the namedrop.

Standing in the way of the vast majority of these gigs was a technical recruiter peddling a mediocre salary, shit insurance, and a 401k that you would only be qualified to participate in once most of the contract was completed. I have only gone directly to a company as a W2 employee twice in my entire career. I'm not sure if my penchant for going through these technical recruiters was a function of where I'd been looking for my next gig (websites) or how efficiently they (the recruiters) reach out to candidates. However it was, I've ended up speaking to hundreds of these recruiters over the course of my career.

And in the span of that career (again, over twenty-five years), I don't think a single one of these interactions has ever led me to believe that they even knew the difference between Java and JavaScript. None of these "technical recruiters" were any bit technical, and yet they were making a fortune in the technology industry by exploiting my (and your) hard-earned knowledge and skills. They don't give a shit about keeping companies staffed with the best in IT tech and keeping the best in IT tech employed at fair rates. These technical recruiting companies are an army of cut-throat middlemen telemarketers whose sole focus every six-to-ten-hour workday is to convince halfwits like me to leave their current steady job for nothing more than an extra five hourly and criminally bad insurance.

When you answer their first call, the single most important thing to know about your adversary is that you might not even be the target they're working to get info on. There's a million reasons to contact you, and hiring is only one of them. They could be trying to learn more about your current employer and any open positions there. They could be trying to get info on your manager, IT director, or current projects. This industry is a hall of mirrors, and you've gotten roped into a game that you didn't even know you were playing.

In this game that we call salary negotiation, you have been firmly cast as its protagonist. And while HR or a recruiting company may act as the antagonist, pointing the finger at them may not place the blame with the correct party. I mean, I wouldn't fault a snake for being a snake the same way that I can't blame a for-profit organization for trying to lower their labor costs and maximize their profits. They aren't really evil. This is anything but emotional to them. This is their job, and they are way more practiced and dissociated with the process. The objectives that they're bringing to the negotiations table do not align with most, if any, of your personal interests.

Ultimately, you have to ask for what you're worth. Ultimately, you have to make the case to support all of the things that you need and want. You're the one responsible for feeding the mouths (creature, kid, or otherwise) at home, keeping that home, and any and all other financial obligations that you may have. The person that you're going up against is not responsible for any of that, and they won't think twice about the salary they got you down to unless it comes up in some profit and loss report. You will always be exponentially more invested in the outcome of this than they will ever be.

It's hard to look at this process as a game if you're between jobs. It's really hard to keep a clear head about it when you have all the preconceptions of the who-what-when-where-why-and-how of a prospective job.

It's a fallacy to conflate the voice over the phone with the company that will actually be writing your checks. You're probably the 50th person they've spoken to that day, and it's best to imagine that they won't remember this conversation beyond their notes in their candidate tracking system, also known as the CTS. But this CTS has perfect memory, and I can promise you that they have a history of every number you have ever said.

So if you're looking for any one key thing to start the fight against their fuckery, here it is: watch, watch, watch what you say to them.

WATCH YOUR MOUTH

What you have to keep in mind is that you are ultimately trying to maximize the amount of money and/or benefits that you possibly can get from each and every negotiation. The ultimate goal of the recruiter, however, is different. They're looking to charge x for you, pay you y, and get the largest delta between those two variables as possible. The objective of getting the lowest rate tends to take precedence over getting the best candidate for the position.

Which, considering that the vast majority of recruiters hadn't entered the market to put the perfect candidate in the perfect position, makes sense. They are driven by the hard, bottom-line numbers. They started a sales job that dictated from the very beginning that their operating rules are made only to maximize corporate profits by putting butts in seats. These recruiters are devouring the industry that they had not invented, innovated, or expanded. They are the middlemen that end up driving entire industries out from the country that made them.

And when they think they smell a chance to scam, these weasels tend to have pretty impeccable memory in all the worst ways. Any information you give them could potentially come to fuck you over. Every single word that comes out of your mouth can and probably will be used down the road. So, unless it benefits you in any way, just keep it to yourself. For example, it doesn't seem like there's much harm in admitting that you're looking to change jobs, right? You do that, and the recruiter's next call might be to let an account manager know that there's a position opening up. Yes, it's very often like *that*.

Like I've said, this whole thing is a game that you probably didn't even see that you were playing. Now that you know, though, you hopefully want to win. But, what does winning look like here?

A couple things: a good gig, the best rate you can get, benefits that are actually beneficial, things like that. The goal of this book is to teach you how to get that total victory. At the bare minimum, though, you can call yourself a winner if you avoid getting totally fucked.

We'll start with not getting fucked.

CHAPTER TWO: ALL ABOUT RECRUITERS

TLDR:

- Recruiters exist because companies have failed to develop efficient in-house hiring processes.
- Recruiters can and will try to fuck you over for just about anything.
- Recruiters typically fall into two categories: one is actively looking to gain something at your expense, while the other is just quick and careless with their candidate search/placement. Both will put you in bad situations.
- The honest recruiter does exist. However, they are too rare to expect to encounter in the field.
- Anything you ever say to a recruiter is going to be recorded into their Candidate Tracking System, or CTS.
- The personalities attracted to IT tech are often naive and too trusting of recruiters. Most people have to learn the hard way. Save yourself the pain

and always practice caution with any and all
recruiters, no matter how "nice" they may seem.

RECRUITERS: The Origin Story

Given that they don't seem to add much value into our
industry or employment prospects, I think it's pretty fair to ask:
why the fuck do we even have recruiters?

Recruiters exist for a couple of reasons, but it ultimately
boils down to their reach, speed, and supposedly "reliable"
technical screening process. But, you might be wondering,
couldn't the company that's actually looking for a hire do this
themselves? Let's take a look.

Here's a simple hypothetical: a company is looking to hire a
software developer. The company is looking to find this person
in the greater Orlando area, which has a population of roughly
2.6 million people. Of those 2.6 million-ish people, it's no
stretch to suppose that at least one of them would be qualified
for the position.

Now, let's get a little more specific. Say the company is
looking for this person to have experience with Angular, C#,
and AWS. I used my favorite, expensive PID tool that
LinkedIn offers to search for people who would fit this bill.
This search returned about 115 people in the greater Orlando
area who have listed these skills on their LinkedIn profile. So,
out of those 2.6 million-ish people, we have about 115 here that
could actually be considered. Considering that we only need to
find 1 out of those 115, the pool is still pretty good.

But that's assuming that all of those 115 people are looking
for a job. With their skillset, most of them are likely to be (somewhat) happily employed. How many of them do you think
would actually consider a new position? We'll take a wild guess

and suppose it's something like 7-15% of them, depending on the currents of the job market. That now leaves us with anywhere between 8 to 17 people out of that 115. Still, since we're only trying to find just one, this seems doable.

Of those 8 to 17 people, though, are any of them actually competent? It goes without saying, but a lot of people that look good on paper fail to carry that impression in person. How many do you think can even program their way out of a paper bag? Five? Two? Any?

The search would then probably have to be expanded statewide or even across the entire country to find that one person. And when you're looking broader, you of course run into the trouble of finding someone who's qualified *and* would be willing to relocate. This process would go on and on and on and on...

Allow me to remind you that this is obviously not a company's only task or something that an HR department is even set up to do. So many other things are going on at the same time that a seemingly simple process turns into an incredibly tedious and drawn-out affair. This isn't like putting a "Now Hiring" sign up in your storefront window and having some kid walk in with a resume that day; this really is that needle-in-the-haystack kind of search.

Here's where the appeal (and, yes, even *value*) of a recruiting company comes in. They could probably reach out to 60-80% of the entire talent pool, and they could do it in less than a week. Remember that out of that potential 115, the amount of them that are looking for a job and would actually apply is very, very few. When a company is looking at those limited prospects, it'd make sense for them to outsource to a service that promises to deliver qualified candidates, and to send them over *fast*.

And *fast* is their biggest selling point. Recruiting companies apparently do have a process to weed through candidates and pick someone competent. The reliability of this supposed process is questionable, but I can speak to its speed. If you want somebody, they really will get you somebody. Now if that person turns out to be a dumbass not worth even their desk-space, that tends to be your problem.

Fast seems to be about the only thing that they're geared toward. Their technical interviews are built for speed over accuracy. Their mysterious process could best be described as a series of wide, haphazard nets they fling out to filter people for reasons that they don't even understand themselves.

Something that happens way too often is that a technical recruiting organization will force the candidates that they've gotten employed to do the screenings without any guidance. The result of this is that you're getting screened by someone who is 1.) not trained to do this and 2.) probably aren't getting even paid to do it. Think about it: many or most of the recruiter's technical employees are hourly workers. They're doing this outside of work at the request of the recruiter that got them their current job. The time that they spend screening you is most likely not getting added to their paycheck. With all this considered, do you think they know or really care about what they're doing?

If companies ever figured out a reliable way to screen, to reach out to even 60% of the talent pool and gave the leeway to pay 30% more for the worthy candidates, then they could accomplish all (and more) that a recruiting company does. But most companies that employ technical people have yet to invest in the processes necessary to properly screen their candidates. Lacking these much-needed processes means that companies have ended up hiring some truly horrible people, and they did it at the cost of an exorbitant amount of time and money. It's for this reason that recruiters exist. You might as well just get used to them, too. Given the current system, recruiters are probably going to be around for a while.

WHAT THEY DO

Throughout my career, I have witnessed these "technical" recruiters doing the most underhanded and low-life business practices that you'd otherwise attribute to meth dealers. I've seen recruiters put someone at a company and, once they'd gone full-time, turn around and hire them away for another contract not even a month later. I've seen recruiters hire someone for one rate and then lower it once that person had already quit their job, since they knew that they would have few other options other than to just take it.

While working at Disney, I once had a recruiter calling from a national firm to offer me a downright stupid amount of money to leave my then-current job for a different one in town. This should've sent off all of the alarm bells in my head, as recruiters very rarely lead with the money, but greed pushed me to actually consider it. I met up with him at a sushi place close to the office. Tanner (obviously not his real name) was only in his twenties, yet he pulled up in a new BMW, an expensive suit, and twitched like his afternoon's 20mg of Adderall hadn't quite kicked in. I could clock this kid as a special kind of sociopath before he even got out of the parking lot. While I tried to enjoy my eel, he tried to build a compelling case as to why I should take the position. He was practicing his own Bateman-esque idea of "charm" all the while, which meant that he talked about four inches from my face and forced unbreaking eye contact as I ate.

Midway through lunch was when he switched gears into asking about my current job: the position, my boss, coworkers, any projects that I was working on, etc. If we hadn't been sitting in some nameless little Japanese restaurant, standard cherry blossom screens and fountains by the door, I would have sworn that I was in an interrogation.

After lunch, he gave me one of those insincere hand-shake/should-squeeze things that are just weird for everyone, and then we went off on our separate ways. It occurred to me on the drive back to my office that something felt a bit off, but it wasn't until a few days later that I got the confirmation that the whole encounter was actually some kind of phishing expedition.

Because a few days later, my boss called me into her office to "talk". She'd heard that I was about to leave my position. As we were coming toward a critical point in our current project, she obviously didn't appreciate my apparent timing of it all.

Now, take a wild guess as to where she heard this from.

The same twitchy Tanner that'd taken me out for sushi had then turned around and set up a lunch with my boss to let her know that I was about to up and quit. But, not to worry, as he had a perfect replacement that would even work at a lower rate. Luckily, I was able to quickly clear up the misinformation with my boss and manage to keep my job.

I still have no idea what Tanner aimed to accomplish. Was he trying to somehow get me fired and personally take my job? Did he want to get in my department? Was this his idea of worming a way into the company? My best guess is that he was just so self-seeking that my possible fate never registered as even a single thought in that gelled, chemically-wired head of his.

So, the one clear thing about that entire encounter was only that he was not concerned with me. I was but a means to carry out some crackpot idea that he'd concocted that, in one of those rarely fair instances of the universe, Tanner never managed to see through. I stayed at that position until we finished the project and Tanner failed to place anyone, himself or otherwise, in my department.

Tanner was not just some anomaly experience. I've had a million different recruiters try to con me in a million different ways: to take a shit job, into a shit rate, I've even had other recruiters try to pump me for information under the guise of an interview. Tanner and the rest of them had actively looked to fuck me over, but they were hardly the worst that I've come across. The worst was only out of carelessness, but still managed to cost me multiple potential employment opportunities and personally put me in a bind.

The worst of the (very) worst:

I don't mean to divulge into too many personal stories, but since this one pretty aptly demonstrates just about every grievance a technical recruiter can make, I'll go ahead and tell you all about a company that I had the misfortune to come across a couple of years back.

Some background: I was closing out a contract that'd run a little too long for my liking, and I was starting to get nervous about the coming "dead zone" of hiring. This dead zone is at about the final quarter of the year, when the appetite for hiring pricey people is as low as the remaining IT budgets.

So given my situation, I was a bit more receptive than usual when this company contacted me about a gig at a finance organization in Orlando. They said they even had *several* possible contracts available, and that they wanted a current copy of my resume. I'd never worked for this organization prior, but I was admittedly enticed by the $60+ hourly that they were offering. My typical rate at the time was anywhere from $50-$75 an hour, depending on the work and longevity of the contract. But work availability tends to decrease toward the end of the year as the budgets get spent up, and so their offer seemed good enough to follow up on.

I sent over my resume with a preface asking the recruiter to check with me before submitting it off to a company, as I already had a few irons in the fire and didn't want to risk getting sent twice. I got an email back a couple of days later. The recruiter's reply wasn't to ask permission to send my resume off, but rather to say that he had a client who was interested. This rang the alarms for a couple of reasons: he never did a skills check, we never spoke about any specific company, and he completely ignored my request that he ask before submitting.

I immediately called this guy up and asked him why the Hell he had sent out my resume without consent. He tried to pacify my (justified) irritation by saying that I would be perfect for his banking client offering a $150k annual and that he was going to call me with more details within the next few days. At this point I already knew that he was full of shit, but I still decided to soldier on with the ghost of a hope that he was actually going to get me a gig.

Over the following couple of weeks, I came to realize that this fucking guy wasn't going to be doing that. What he *did* do, though, was blast my resume to every single hiring employer in the area. Now, this might not be too egregious of an error in another industry. But in the IT world, employers absolutely hate getting the same resume twice. That's an immediate cast-aside for them, as they never want to be involved in a conflict between two technical recruiters. The employer can never really know who is already under contract and even what possible employment laws they would be breaking to hire the candidate, so it's easiest to just write that candidate off entirely.

So, since this recruiter had sent my resume to every hiring manager in town, I was effectively put in a permanent "reserve" for the few contracts left at the end of the year. Every time I was submitted by another recruiter, the company would reply back that I had already been sent over, and nothing ever went further from there. The result of all this bullshit was that I could not find a new contract until the following year. In one careless act, this recruiter kept me from actually getting employed *at all*.

Let's be clear about where you stand in the technology industry: you are either working for a classic employer, playing the recruiter's game, or creating your very own game. Contracting can bring home 25-50% more than most full-time jobs and might grant the kind of freedom that most rat-racers dream can only dream of. But recruiters have the inside track to certain industries and, in those industries, the only way to the job is through one of them. They're the ones that hold the channel, regardless of whatever dirty way that they got it, to the managers looking for your skills. And they have the reach, funding, and patience that most people simply cannot afford.

In this way, most of us have to come to a begrudging acceptance of the recruiter. They are a sort of necessary evil in our industry. Not that all recruiters are evil, of course. At the end of the day, though, they have priorities that tend to come into conflict with your own. However nice they may sound over the phone or even at a business lunch, you cannot let yourself forget the ultimate fact: they don't really have your best interests in mind.

THEIR BOTTOM LINE

In my time as a potential recruit, I've been presented with coding interview clichés in hundreds of ways by hundreds of people that hadn't had a clue what they were even talking about to begin with. Quick example: the difference between a bubble sort and a quicksort, or between an abstract class and an interface. Recruiters don't comprehend what they're asking you any further past what's written on the tired list of coding questions handed to them by their pit bosses within the boiler room Hell that they work.

What they are ultimately looking for is the shortest path possible to allow them to submit your resume to a client. If that means reading off a bunch of shit that they can't understand, then so be it. If that might mean telling you whatever you might want to hear, sure. And if that means blasting your resume off without any indication that you are actually qualified for the job, then that's just hunky-fucking-fine by them.

Because they are salespeople that sell people, and the sooner they can get enough resumes to send over, the better. It's essential to understand that these are not technology organizations so much as they are sales organizations/scam artists. Once you, the actual technology professional, can see past those glossy logos and technical service offerings and see them for what they are, you'll be able to start to actually navigate your next salary.

Please note: with all this said, I still have to admit that there really does exist the rare good person who is trying to do the right thing in a very deceitful industry. They're much easier to identify because they tend to take their time to actually speak with you and seem almost embarrassed to ask what your current salary is. Also, they tend to go to their max rate when pressed enough. Again, unfortunately, I must also reiterate that the good ones are *rare*, and you're not likely to encounter one very often.

INTO THE WOLF'S Den and Onto My Soapbox

Years ago, I had the pleasure of actually visiting a large technical recruiting center. It was a high-pressure boiler room, sure, but it seemed more like a *Glengarry Glen Ross* simulation than a technology company. A ping-pong table and an Xbox sat off from a fully-stocked kitchen, but the saleroom itself was a huge, low-walled cube farm. Each morning saw a hype-up session with blasting music to rev up the salespeople, who all looked about thirty at the max. These kids reminded me of pharma reps, or maybe 90s stockbrokers: young, good-looking, dressed sharp, and making way less money than they would ever care to admit. They each had a quota of people to contact and/or harass every day, and they were looking to make it. The place just reeked of the high-fiving, shit-talking, frat-kid-turned-salesman-type that used "bro" as a verbal punctuation. The whole affair left a bad taste in my mouth, but it could've just been from all the Axe spray.

But it did make me realize a few things. There was absolutely no way in Hell that these people had any idea as to the quality of a candidate's skill beyond what was claimed on their resume. Not that that really mattered to them, though, because there was also no chance that the quality of the candidate was their top priority. That was the task, I remind you, for which they were pulling in egregious sums of money from their clients to help identify. These recruiters are nothing but a sales machine that can cast a wide net, and they can only be trusted to further their own interests over yours or even of the business that they apparently work for. Period.

Have you ever stopped to notice that about 90% of the job ads on LinkedIn, Monster, Dice, Career Builder, etc. are from technical recruiters? They've cornered the market as the de facto middlemen between potential employees and the companies that don't have the time or manpower to find the candidates on their own (which, in case you may not have realized, is a *lot* of companies).

But one of the main things about recruiters, other than their ruthless nature, is that they're ultimately in a hurry. The daily call quotas exist to get you added to their sales pipeline. They will compress a truly staggering amount of info into only a couple of minutes, once they can keep you on the call. What you have to do here is not to take anything personally and keep an eye on your own objectives. They've got a thorough checklist back on their end to make a dossier on you, your skills, your aspirations, and anything else that they may find of value (not to mention to the other 100+ who'll inevitably call you back from that firm).

This dossier that they'll build up on you is only one of the countless in their candidate tracking system, or CTS, as it's known in the industry lingo. No information is ever wasted, and the details of just about every conversation that you've ever had with a recruiter has been documented (even if somewhat poorly) into a CTS. The one thing that they'll always take special care to note is every single salary requirement that you have ever mentioned, and this collective memory works as an invaluable advantage for them in negotiations. Ever wondered why they always seem to ask very similar, if not even exactly the same questions? Questions about where you're currently working or the name of your supervisor? While all of these questions may seem more or less innocuous, this is actually rather purposeful probing for intel on you and your current employment that they use for later exploitation.

My favorite question has got to be the incredibly audacious: "How much do you make?" I mean, can you imagine the kind of brass that it'd take to call a stranger and outright ask them their salary? Is there any other industry where that would be okay, let alone *normal*? Recruiters are near-literal wolves that prey on the naturally trusting nature of technology people. They're betting on you to assume that they have all the best intentions. And, of course, most of us usually do trust that others are good until proven otherwise. We don't jump to think that they're trying to screw us. We just get confused. How many times have you wondered *just what in the Hell was that all about* after getting off the phone with one of them?

Well, now you know. Most people in our industry have to have several bad encounters before they come to understand this. You can save yourself so much potential pain if you accept the fact now that a recruiter is not really here to help you and to act as though they come with a warning label: EXERCISE EXTREME CAUTION WHEN INTERACTING WITH THESE MEN AND WOMEN. Do this, and you'll never have to learn the hard way.

CHAPTER THREE: UNDERSTANDING THE MATH

<u>TLDR:</u>

- The rate that you would ask for is a lot less than the rate that you really need.
- The rate always works out to be less once you factor in the variables of the actual job.
- You need to take taxes, insurance, time-off, commute, etc. into account when calculating your rate.
- Being a salaried employee often translates into working more for less than you would've made if you were paid hourly.
- A 1099 is usually more beneficial for an employer than an employee.
- Anything and everything that affects what goes into your pocket should be factored into your rate. These factors can be used to ask and argue for more.

YOU'RE Naive and You Know It

Avoiding any self-congratulation, but it takes a very specific (some would even say *special*) type of person to work in the technology industry. We have spent the entirety of our careers learning, preparing, and practicing for what we do. Try to count all of the hours spent figuring out how to develop modern web applications or trying to understand the many complexities of network security. Not everyone is cut out to transpile Type-Script, or figure JavaScript package management, GIT, encryption, network security, SQL, or any other part of the dizzying array of intricate systems that we somehow manage to write, administrate, rescue, or secure.

Some of us may have caught the technology bug after getting a Commodore VIC-20, Atari 400, or an Amiga for Christmas. Others might have simply seen a webpage do something amazing and felt compelled to dive into the HTML to figure out how it all worked. You either started out on this technology trek because you were following the money, or you had realized later on that people would actually pay you for the thing that you'd already been doing in your spare time. For passion or paycheck, you have dedicated enormous amounts of time to learn and master the things that most people can't even understand.

But at no point did your teachers, parents, professors, confidants, or anyone else ever teach you how to negotiate a single damn thing. We are nerds and, by nature, pretty conflict-averse. And the very nature of negotiation is a conflict, or at least feels that way to the more sensitive among us. Have you ever said a rate that, the moment those numbers left your mouth, you knew was too low? It's almost as if you don't want to let the other person down, or you don't want to seem too greedy. Whatever the reason, it all comes down to your lack of negotiating experience or training.

To make it even worse, you're probably going into negotiations without any real information on the position or project. Oh, and I did mention that you are usually going up against a trained professional, right? If you go into this without any preparation, you're fucked from the minute you pick up the phone. They'll do whatever they can to lock you down on a number, as recruiters know that the earlier that they can get you to commit to a rate, the better.

This isn't fair for a couple of reasons. First, the less you know about the gig, the less you will probably ask for to do it. Does it change anything for you to know that the job requires a daily two-hour commute? Will you have to manage people, or is this just a heads-down coding gig? Is insurance going to cost you an extra $1,500 a month? Do you get any paid vacation, or is it just straight work time? How long will the gig last? Is it going to be a short contract, or are you looking at a long-term salaried position? Depending on the answer, any single one of these questions could potentially tack on another $10k to what you are asking for, and the recruiter that called you in the middle of the workday knows this fact way more than they'll ever let on.

You might not know what even your most *basic* rate is, with no other special aspects included. How much do you need to live? How much do you think you need to make? Mark it down. Look at that number. Does it seem right? Alright.

Would your number hold up if we were to look at it any closer? As in, to break that hypothetical down in the realities of a workplace?

The most important thing you can have going into negotiations is *information*, and the first thing that you need to get is a good base knowledge of salary. The number they offer rarely works out to really be that number, and this chapter will give a breakdown of why that is and why you always *need* to push for more.

HOURLY BASICS

Right off the bat, you are going to be at a major disadvantage if you don't understand the math that goes into calculating hourly rates or a yearly salary. I cannot overstate just how important it is that you understand rate calculation. Your adversary knows and uses a few tricks to bend what you may consider to be a good figure, and this knowledge is going to help you combat that.

ON HOURLY RATES

The best way to figure out an estimated yearly rate is to take your proposed hourly rate and multiply it by the total working days per year. If you worked every available day in the year, this would be the hourly rate times the approximately 2,080 possible working hours out of the year, which is simply just a 40-hour workweek by 52 weeks.

Hourly rates can be somewhat tricky, as you need to be able to calculate your yearly salary so that you have something to compare it to. For example, fifty dollars an hour has no real meaning to you in the grand scheme of things because it ultimately all comes down to the yearly salary. Hourly rates will not give you any good basis for comparing last year to this one. Without a good grasp on this, you won't know if you're actually getting a good rate or deal.

Let's go ahead and take a rate of fifty dollars per hour. In order to estimate your gross income (refresher: that's your raw income before taxes or insurance), you just have to take

50 (hourly rate) x 2080 (available working hours out of the year) = 104,000

...which means that you can expect to receive about $104,000 for the year prior to paying taxes and insurance.

But the thing is, you're probably not going to get to work all of those 2,080 hours during the year. You are going to get sick. You are going to leave early for your daughter's piano recital. You are going to (hopefully) take a vacation. With all this considered, you're more than likely going to end up working about 1,960 hours (that's three weeks off out of the year) if everything goes absolutely perfectly. So now that $104k is starting to look really more like $98k for the year.

Now, you're not even going to be taking home that $98,000. Do you live in a country? Then unless you want to one day end up getting all of your assets seized or going to jail, you're going to need to pay taxes. Your tax bracket is dependent on your income, but it's safe to say that the majority of us are going to be in about the midrange. We'll go ahead and translate this to be about a thirty-percent cut out of your income. This percentage can vary a bit based on your state. For ease of calculation, let's just suppose that they'll be taking about a third of your annual salary.

So now you're at about $68,600 for the year. That figures to about a $2,800 paycheck every other week. Oh, but you must need insurance, right? That's going to be about another $500 to even $2,200 a month, depending on the greed of your employer and the number of people that you need to insure. On the lowest end, that's another $6,000 out of your annual. That takes you down to a $62,600 salary, or a $2,407 bimonthly paycheck.

Does that $50 hourly really seem sufficient now?

. . .

LET'S REVIEW

Hourly rate: $50

Available working hours out of the year (with three weeks off): 1,960

Gross income: hourly rate*annual hours

$50*1,960= $98,000

Approximated tax rate: 30%

Net income: gross income- (tax rate*gross income)

$98,000*(0.3*$98,000) = $68,600

Weekly paycheck: net income/weeks in the year

$68,600/52= $1,319.23

Biweekly paycheck: weekly paycheck*2

$1,319.23*2= $2,638.46

So now when it comes to negotiating a fair hourly rate, you have actual figures to compare to what they're offering.

A NOTE on 1099 v W2

Before I risk talking out of my ass, allow me to reiterate that I am a nerd. This in no way, shape, or form makes me a lawyer or an account, nor does it give me any of their credentials. Still, it is incredibly important to understand the difference between 1099 and W2, and so I will try to give you the best explanation that I am qualified to give.

A W2 employee is very much that: an *employee*, and entitled to everything that comes with that position. Working as a 1099 most essentially means that you are a consultant, freelancer, independent contractor, etc., and you have no claim to the benefits that would normally entail with a W2. When it comes to insurance, a retirement plan, and everything else, you're pretty much on your own.

The biggest difference between a W2 and a 1099 is that the responsibility of reporting income and paying taxes falls solely on a 1099. A W2 typically receives their paychecks with everything already deducted and can sometimes even look to receiving a yearly tax return. Someone working on a 1099 contract has to set aside money to pay taxes yearly or even quarterly.

The benefits of working on a W2 are pretty obvious. The advantages of a 1099 seem to almost only be for the employer, as they get to push the burden of figuring out taxes and insurance onto the person that they've hired. This way, the company can just pay the person to do the work that needs to be done without getting monetarily tied to that person like they would with a proper employee. If a W2 can be equated to a committed relationship, then the 1099 is a "no-strings-attached".

There is one advantage for the worker that most people don't tend to consider. When you file a 1099, you are able to write off a *lot* of stuff as a business expense. Check with an accountant, of course, but anything that you bought and used to do the job can be accepted for a tax deduction. But aside from this, it usually works out to be much more beneficial to get on as a W2 rather than a 1099. If you're working somewhere like an employee would, it's well within your rights to ask to be treated like an employee, too.

ALL THINGS CONSIDERED

Knowing how much you really need to live and the differences between pay structure/contracts will help you in a couple of ways. First of all, it'll help you to figure out how much you need to ask for, especially in respect to whether you're going to be hourly/salary or 1099/W2. Second, the other side is betting on you to not understand how the pay will actually work out. Showing them different is only going to better your case in asking for—and getting—what you really need.

CHAPTER FOUR: HOW TO TALK TO RECRUITERS

TLDR:

- "The First Contact Ceremony" refers to when a recruiter initially reaches out about potential employment.
- The ceremony is going to more-or-less follow this sequence: the contact, an availability probe, and an attempt at establishing interest.
- Recruiters will occasionally call you under the pretense of a First Contact Ceremony, but they may actually be attempting to scam you for information.
- While on this call, remember to be polite but to stay guarded. Decline to answer any questions that aren't relevant to the gig that they're pitching you.
- These "technical" recruiters don't know shit about our industry. Do not try to talk technical with them, and do not call them out on their lack of technical knowledge.

- The most successful method of communication with recruiters is usually over email or messaging rather than over the phone.

FIRST CONTACT CEREMONY

Before we go too far too quick, we have to put the (very) first things first: that initial call from the recruiter. Every first call has a certain predictable ceremony. They are all essentially the same, with just a few deviations that I will expand on later. Every other part of these "ceremonies" are pretty much the same. If you can remember a few essential rules, then you can consider yourself well-prepared for any and all possible calls.

First: always be polite, as nobody wants to work with an asshole. This may seem like a simple statement, if not incredibly obvious, but a lot of people could benefit from this reminder. I myself am actually a bit of an asshole, and I am not alone. It seems to be a relatively common character flaw. There are, after all, a lot of assholes in the world, and it's reasonable to expect that at least a few of us are going to be ones as well.

But you can't be an asshole where it counts. I mean, you should want to always keep it in check, but especially here. If you come off rude over the phone, there probably will not be a call back.

As previously mentioned, never give away any information that does not directly benefit you. Be friendly (see section above) but guarded. This call may not be about you at all. The recruiter could be calling only to phish for information on your current job. Don't take anything personally, but there always stands a chance that the free lunch they're taking you to may really be about getting to your manager or director that they've been eyeing as a new contact. Pro tip: if you look the "recruiter" up on LinkedIn and their listed title is "account manager", then you, my friend, are almost certainly being taken for a ride.

The only purpose for this kind of contact is to try to gather a little inside intel, with the ultimate goal of getting a new contact within your current company. If they straight-up just ask you who your current manager or superior is, then that should put you on high alert.

Also, congratulations! At this point, I think even the most optimistic of you readers may be starting to realize how sleazy this industry actually is. It really is its own little Wild West out here where, unfortunately, we are not the cowboys so much as we are the cows.

Most recruiters will have a list of questions that they look to affix answers to. Some apply to hiring you, and some apply to opening new accounts. Either way, the bottom line is to be kind and be courteous, but to always be especially aware of each and every word that comes out of your mouth.

THE CONTACT

The initial greeting prompted from an email will later result in a call. If the initial contact was the call, then this will start right into a basic introduction from the recruiter. Listen closely, as you need to figure out the real purpose of their call. (Extremely carefully) feeding them bits and pieces of information can work as an excellent chip to barter with, as they may even have information that you could find useful.

THE AVAILABILITY PROBE

At this point, the recruiter is simply trying to determine whether to add or remove you from the list of people that they can move further through the process. I've personally had them outright ask early on in the call if I would be willing to listen to potential opportunities. It might seem like another way to waste your time, but you should actually always say yes to this. There is always at least *something* to learn from them.

In this part of the call, you have the opportunity to practice your negotiations skills, learn the market rate, or to figure out exactly what skills are paying at the moment. Remember: you are always and forever on the market, even when you aren't. If you lose touch with the currents in the industry, then you risk entering negotiations without all the essential information such as present going rates and the sought-after skills.

ATTEMPT AT ESTABLISHING Interest

The recruiter will then begin pitching their opening(s), all the while trying to gauge your level of actual interest. They are going to do anything they can to hype up the value of the people/place/project, as they are also trying to move the value off of the actual rate that they'll offer.

That's not to say that they won't talk numbers. Once they see that they might have your attention, they're going to try to go in for an early kill and throw out some range to see if you're on board with it. It makes sense on their end to check that you're even in their ballpark, but you should be cautious with how you answer this. It could limit your options later on when you get closer toward the final sit-down. If you agree that your rate is between x and y without knowing exactly what the job entails, then you're not going to have much wiggle room if you end up needing to ask for more.

You are never their only target. A recruiter is typically calling, messaging, friending, hounding, harassing, and talking to countless other potential candidates every single day of the week. As a result, they're going to minimize the effort that they put into each and every interaction. Again, they're about quantity over quality, but that doesn't mean that they don't still have themselves ready to fuck you over at the first chance.

Even though recruiters aren't putting too much effort into you, you still need to tread carefully with them. Navigating their verbal minefield is our next lesson.

HOW TO TALK to Recruiters

Unless you are somehow a self-sustaining hermit in the woods, you have had to learn some social skills in order to navigate the world with fellow humans. From your first attempt at talking to this morning's coffee run, your ability to interact with others has come to influence your success more than you might realize.

We all know the basics: smiling, the importance of "please" and "thank you", how to hold the elevator. But then comes all of the social nuances, those little things that just might not come as easily to the same personality types that are drawn into IT tech.

We're not going to worry ourselves about the intricacies. I can't teach you interpersonal intelligence, and that doesn't really matter here. Here, we're just going to try to lay out only what you absolutely need to know: how to talk to recruiters.

BE POLITE

As previously stated, no one wants to work with an asshole. As previously stated, this is something I have to work on myself. The basic rules help. Be polite. Use your manners. You don't want to be an asshole, or at least come off as one over the phone.

What you want to come off as is someone that's worth

anyone's potential time/money/help. For anybody else on the Asshole Spectrum, this is not exactly an easy-peasy task. If you're not so good on the phone, I've personally found opening the phone dialogue in this way to be more than helpful:

Recruiter: Hello, may I speak to Scott?

Me: Hello, this is Scott.

Recruiter: My name is Chad, and I am looking for a blah blah blah...

Me: Hi Chad, I'm a little nervous on the phone, so please don't take my silence for rudeness. I promise you, I don't mean anything by it.

And just like that, you've earned some immediate understanding from the caller! Anyone who isn't an absolute monster will be happy to work with you when you are upfront and honest in this manner. They may even go so far as to work a little harder to help you out.

Always be polite, even when the person calling you up hasn't earned it. You don't have to meet assholery on their end with rudeness on yours. Some people get so hung up in the social contract when it comes to these niceties. Quit. Remember: this is a game, and the whole point of it is to win. You're not even going to meet the other person on the phone a majority of the time, so who really cares how polite or rude they are? Regardless of how they may treat you on the phone, stay polite and stay calm. Even if it becomes clear that they're not going to hook you up to a gig, then you can at least ask them about rate info and the general market conditions. Everyone has some useful information and all you have to do is ask for it.

BUT DON'T Talk Technical

I've got a bit of a shocker for you: technical recruiters are almost never actually technical. In fact, I can say for certain that I haven't ever met a technical technical recruiter in the entirety of my career. Like I've said, these people don't even know the difference between Java and JavaScript, and it shows.

Problem is, they don't want you to know that fact. They also think that they can somehow hide their complete lack of knowledge in the industry that they've built their entire careers on exploiting. So oftentimes when you speak with a technical recruiter they will try to fake some "know-how", and the results are about as poor as you would expect. What you can usually expect to hear is a misplaced marketing major attempting to pass themselves off as an expert in your field, and this can be both hilarious and somewhat insulting to hear.

But holy shit, you *cannot* let them know that. If you want to maximize your relationship with the recruiter, you can't get in any way smug or arrogant over the fact that they sound like an idiot. Yes, they don't know the difference between Java and JavaScript, but telling them this is not going to be doing you any favors. Us nerds can get pretty egocentric in our areas of expertise, and it's natural to almost feel a little hostile towards others that claim to be like us (but aren't).

Should technical recruiters at least know a *little* about the field that they're putting candidates in? Yes, and it ought to be downright embarrassing for them that their ignorance has come to be basically an industry standard. But you make that your personal bone to pick, and it's going to come at the expense of employment opportunities. Don't. It's just not worth it.

Talk to them like you'd talk to someone who's completely outside of the industry. Avoid any insider jargon. If they use (read: misuse) any technical lingo, forgive it and leave it. Get at what they actually know: the gigs.

THE BEST WAY TO "TALK"

You're probably already aware of this, but the telephone isn't the only method of communication. It really isn't even one of the main channels anymore. Most people prefer just about anything else over the face-to-face or voice-to-voice. Text, email, and LinkedIn all obviously exist, and they're all perfectly acceptable channels to get and keep in contact with a recruiter.

Using a method that doesn't require live real-time communication may actually be your best choice for a couple of reasons. First, let's talk about the IT type. I am annoyingly outgoing and sociable, but most engineers are not. Most of us don't really like talking to people, especially strangers, especially strangers trying to sell you at a cut-rate. You might find yourself much more relaxed and composed when you can type out and edit your every word.

Being able to take the time to write and send your messages will help keep your overall communication as precise as possible. Your fingers can't fumble over a keyboard and accidentally let something slip the way that your mouth will. Recruiters tend to be really great at throwing lots and lots of words into your ear until they fluster you enough to get info, but you're safe from that off of the phone.

While they can't force anything out of you over written communication, you conversely stand a better chance at success in asking the hard questions this way. On the phone, they might be able to dance around your question until it's dropped entirely. You'll hear them go on and on about the pool table in the company's break room, but you won't get to know about the insurance like you'd asked about in the first place. They can't do this so easily over a point-blank message. If you're asking a specific question and they respond with a paragraph of tangents, their evasion is going to be embarrassingly obvious.

We're going to be getting more in-depth about *what* exactly you should ask a recruiter to get the most accurate information about a potential job a little down the line. For the ambitious (or the impatient), check out Chapter 5. There's a list of decent probing questions that you can ask to get a good sense of a gig.

Again, no matter what channel of communication that you decide to use, always ensure that you're civil with them. Since a recruiter can't exactly "hear" your tone over a message, it's important that you write and word the text to sound polite and enthusiastic. You might not actually be feeling enthusiastic about it, and that's totally okay. The best part about writing it out is that you don't have to put a lot of work in to fake it like you would over the phone. Adding a couple of exclamation points and positive words will always do the trick.

For example:

"Hi [RECRUITER'S NAME]! That sounds like a great opportunity! I'm definitely interested to hear more about it, so I've got a couple questions for you."

Then, it's best to word the questions so that they don't come as too cold or direct. For example:

"Can you tell me...?"

"Could you send me the info for...?"

"Do you know if...?"

Finally, you'll want to end the message with something polite that also reiterates your need for information. This is as easily accomplished as:

"Please let me know! Thanks."

See if they can try to write their way around your questions. If so, at least you have documented proof that they're doing this, and it should be a red flag about the potential job itself. The more likely outcome, though, is that you'll actually get some information from them. And information, like we'll talk about, is everything.

CHAPTER FIVE: GET THE FACTS FIRST

TLDR:

- You need to gather any and all information about the prospective job before you can calculate a fair asking rate.
- The most organized way to get information about a job is to create a spreadsheet of consistent questions to ask, and to record any and all answers.
- A recruiter is going to try to get your rate before you're ready to give it. Stall them on this while you get them to answer your questions.
- If you're forced to say a number, give them a range with your actual rate on the lower end.
- Recruiters will sometimes go quiet on their end to try to trick you into talking to fill the awkward silence. You have to resist the urge to speak, as you will usually end up saying more than you'd meant to.

- Wording your questions so that they are open-ended will yield you the most information.

ASKING ALL You Can

If you somehow haven't already understood just how careful you need to be when speaking with recruiters, I'll say it again: anything that comes out your mouth can and probably will be used against you. At this stage, their goal is to nail you down to a rate as quickly as they can. They're going to use any and all of the tricks in their book to push you to spit out a number or, worse, to agree to theirs.

You can't make any decent case for a better rate before you've gathered all of the facts. Before you even get into that conversation, you have to make a spreadsheet of questions. Yes, seriously. This chapter is going to give you some strategies for stalling on giving them any specific number, while getting answers for each and every one of your own questions. Note them down. Only once you've gotten all of the information can you even begin to calculate a rate that's actually fair to you.

Is it a little tedious? Maybe. But like I've said, they've built up a dossier on you. They have everything you've ever said on file. This is just one of the few things that you can do to level the playing field, even if just by a little bit.

Skip at your own risk.

WHAT YOU NEED to Ask

Let's start with the most baseline question:

"What will I be doing on a day-to-day basis?"

Sometimes there's a pretty significant discrepancy between the job described and the actual job that you end up with.

Before anything else, you have to understand exactly what the job that you are interviewing for actually is. You may think that the title/responsibilities listed with the position would make it pretty obvious, but there could be one (if not multiple) idiots that have muddled it up along the way.

Recruiters often can't articulate the position past their list of IT buzzwords, and so the intangibles or subtleties that need to be known to find the right person are often lost. Or a hiring manager could have a completely different idea of what it is they need to hire for in the first place. They might only understand that deadlines are getting missed or that department objectives aren't getting met, but they can't see *who* they specifically need to resolve those issues. None of these nuances are getting communicated over to HR or to the recruiter. I can promise you that much.

And as if you don't already have enough shit to do, but it's also on you to work out what the real responsibilities for the job are. This isn't even a quick thing that you can do through the initial phone call, because the recruiter is trying to rush through everything so that they can get your rate. Again, this is why you don't give them one just yet. They continually fail to accurately depict and describe the jobs that they're trying to rope you into, so you're stuck having to do some information-gathering first. Might as well do it on their time.

Stall on the rate question for as long as you possibly can. If the recruiter keeps pressing, you can try to get the recruiter to give you a range (again, don't say any numbers just yet) and then ask them how flexible this range would be for the right person. For example: if the recruiter says that the gig pays between $35 to $48 an hour, your response should be based around the number that you're trying to actually get. You want $50? Ask if they'd be willing to consider someone for a little out of the range. That maximum can probably stretch as far as even \$55 an hour, but that's not what we're after at this point. All you're doing here is making sure they tell you that they can be flexible. Flexibility, whether real or only professed, will come to help you in negotiations later.

You don't have to talk circles around the recruiter to get to this point. I've managed in so many words by throwing out scenarios like this:

"So, say I turn out to be exactly the right person with the skills, experience, and knowledge for this position. Could you be more flexible with the range?"

They're probably going to respond to this hypothetical by asking if the current range offered isn't enough. You can buy a lot of time to stall on that question by simply saying:

"I just don't really understand what the job is yet."

This also works as a great Segway to gather information. Do you have your questions ready? No worries, since I do. I seriously recommend writing down any and all answers that a recruiter gives. You, after all, are not a computer, and you can't trust yourself to accurately remember every single thing that they say.

Questions you need to ask in order to understand the scope of the job:

1.) How big is the team?

2.) Will I be managing anyone?

3.) How are work items communicated?

4.) What's the methodology for trouble or work tickets? Kanban, Waterfall, Agile, or something else?

5.) What's the scrum team type?

6.) Are there going to be daily standups? Weekly? Any?

7.) Who would be my manager? Do they have a LinkedIn profile?

8.) What's the *specific* project that I would be working on, and what's the *specific* role that I would play in its develop-ment/maintenance/etcetera?

9.) Has this team ever been asked/required to work on the weekend or during the night?

10.) How quickly would I be expected to "ramp up" and be able to add value to the team once I've been hired?

11.) Am I going to be on-call?

12.) What is the nature of the company, and how stable are they?

13.) Are they hiring for multiple roles, or just this one?

Asking (and getting a decent answer) to these is going to give you at least some sense of what you'd be doing. However, even if the recruiter is able to answer all of the questions, you have to play it safe and assume that they don't really know. There's a less-than-little chance that they're being less-than-truthful, and you should take everything with an ear cocked for potential bullshit. If you can, push the recruiter to go get the hiring manager to answer some of the more pointed questions. Ultimately, you should be able to get as much information as you can about the job, and to get as much of an understanding about what you could be getting into as possible.

Of course, you won't really know what the work is going to be like for absolute certainty until your very first day, but at least you've done your best to get a sense of the job for what it is. After getting an answer for everything on the list, it's possible that you might come to the conclusion that this job actually sucks and that you'd be miserable if you took it. Now if the situation stands that the job is terrible but that you truly *need* it, then you will probably at least look to getting paid the absolute maximum in exchange for your suffering.

Now imagine how much worse that situation would be if you hadn't known that the job sucked and failed to negotiate accordingly. You could be stuck in something shitty *and* getting paid like shit to boot. That's what the tedium of intel-gathering can save you from.

All of these questions could also affirm that the job would actually be a fitting and/or good position, and you want to take it. Great. But you're not trying to work for the "love of it" now, are you? There are a few things you can ask to understand all of the other specifics that go into the position like pay type, benefits, commute, and other miscellaneous bits that can all help you to better figure out a fair-for-you number.

- How are you getting paid?

Past duties, let's talk about pay. And no, I'm still not at the rate quite yet. The number is one thing, but *how* are you going to be working for it—hourly or salary? Can they tell you how many hours a week that they'll be expecting you to work? Does that include the weekends? Will you be expected to work outside of the office, or can you shut your phone off at the end of the day?

It seems that one of the common American markers of being "established" within your career is to be a salaried employee. Hourly means that they're tracking you for your every second of direct in-office time rather than valuing you for what you bring to the company each and every day, right? Well, let's examine how easily one can fall into what often turns out to be something that I call the "Salary Trap":

So, you get the job. After some back-and-forth, you and the company agree to start you out on an annual $80k. Suppose you work the standard 40 hours a week. Over 52 weeks, this translates to an hourly $38.36. Depending on your position and experience, this is not a bad rate. But what if, as it tends to be the actual case, you're working more than 40 hours a week?

Say you end up working more like 55 hours each week.

This is a pretty modest estimate, if not even low-balling it. I'm sure that you're already aware, but most companies will try to squeeze as much out of your clock as they can. But we'll go ahead and suppose 55 hours a week over the 52 weeks of the year. That brings your rate down to $27.97. That's over a ten-dollar difference, my friend, that they're fucking you out of on the hourly.

That's not even bringing taxes, insurance, etc., into it. And you might end up working even more—60+ hours a week is not an uncommon expectation in most workplaces. How's that annual looking now? Remember, the whole goal is to maximize what you are being paid for your labor. Getting salaried is not going to always get you a bigger biweekly

- What are the benefits?

Whatever your opinion may be about the value of benefits, you need to at least understand them. What do they cover, and who do they cover? Is it just for you, or will you need to find something else for your family? When do they go into effect? You don't want to end up on COBRA for months while working like a covered employee. And when they finally hit, how much are they going to cost you per pay period? Any and all of these questions can be used as easy leverage for a higher rate. The easiest question, though, is simply asking how much the benefits will cost you. Get that number written down, and then use it to ask for more money in exchange later on.

- How's the commute?

Is this gig going to let you work from home, do work *at* home, or are they going to require you to come into the office

100% of the time? If it's a job where you have to physically show up every day, how far is the drive?

Say the office is a bit of a distance from you. Say that translates to a one-hour drive from your house to the office. Just like working insane hours, long commutes are unfortunately quite common in our current workplace culture (which, to be clear, I think fucking sucks). If you're going to spend two hours each day driving just in pursuit of your paycheck, then you will need to account for this time in some way. Your ideally 8-hour workday has now become at least 10. This addition can and absolutely should be used to negotiate your salary.

- Let's talk about the long-term.

You always have to check the stability of a company. If it seems like they're on their last quarter before a complete closure, it's because they are. If you get into the office and everybody's acting like they might not have their job tomorrow, that's because they won't. Start-ups can become fall-downs *fast*. You don't have to scrutinize every little aspect of everything, but listen to anything telling you that this place won't last. You don't want to end up the jackass running down the gangplank to get on the Titanic.

Contract length should always be considered. Suppose that they want to start the contract out for 6 months. Do they intend on fully hiring you after that 6 months, or are you out after that? If they're planning on having you as basically a temp worker, then that means you'll be in need of the next gig in 6 months. You'll have to find a job again, and soon. That takes time for you and should come at a cost to them. Calculate what that number is and add it to your rate.

. . .

WHEN THEY ASK Questions

Like I've said, the recruiter will start in on their questions within the first phone call. Like I've said, their questions aren't to get to know you better. They don't give a shit. They're just trying to nail a price down on you. You already know this, of course, and you also need to know how to walk that thin line of feeding them just enough information to keep them on the phone without giving them anything that they could actually use as leverage against you.

The best way to go about learning to manage this balance is to first start by learning when you need to shut the fuck up. Have you ever had an awkward lull in a conversation where they go quiet and you feel weird about it, so you keep babbling and accidentally overshare? So has everyone else. It's a universally human thing to feel that intense unease when a silence falls. You feel like you have to fill it out of courtesy or just to pacify your own discomfort—don't. In another situation, you might end up talking about Grandpa's open-casket or something. That'd be embarrassing, but mostly without any later consequence. Here, you might accidentally give them something they shouldn't have (like, God forbid, even a *number*). So when the silence happens, sit with it.

They know what they're doing when they do it. The pausing, the quiet on their line. It's a psychological prompt to get you to fill the void with things that you don't want them to know. Recruiters take tactics from professional interrogators just to try to get you stuck to a number. But as long as you're aware of this, then they don't stand too much of a chance to trick you. They are of an especially slimy breed, true, but that doesn't make them necessarily *smart*.

Here's all you really have to do: don't. When they stop talking as a way to get you to start talking, just let that lull ride. They're not actually interrogators. They can't stare you down and point a lamp in your eyes until you crack like in some cheesy crime drama. You'll come to notice that if they pause during conversations and you don't pick it back up, then they will just start talking again.

I know it will feel really awkward at first. After all, it's going against a part of human nature. We've all been conditioned to continue a conversation at any cost. But here, you have to fight that urge. Remember: never divulge information unless it's to your benefit. Also remember: don't be an asshole. You can be polite while still withholding information. Saying nothing can (and should) be done with a smile.

Not to say that you don't say *anything*. You, of course, still need to talk. That's how a conversation goes. Just make sure that whatever comes out of your mouth won't end up coming back to hurt you. If you're a total newbie in the field, you might be getting a little nervous right now. Feeling like any word you say could turn into a weapon? Wary to even pick up the phone? You don't necessarily have to rake your tongue. Just keep this list in mind when you get on the line. This stuff will 100% fuck up your chance at the job or in later negotiations.

1.) Don't badmouth your current or past employers. We all know someone who talks shit behind everyone's backs. We all know to keep them at a distance. Why? Because common wisdom dictates that if they talk about them to you, then they'll talk about you to them. Same idea in the workplace. They'll throw your resume in the trash before you're even done.

2.) If there's any particular reason you were let go, leave it out unless it somehow makes you look good. Saying that you were offered more at another company and hired away is something that I would think on. You obviously want to go where the money is, but you also don't want to appear in any way flighty to them. Things like layoffs, company closure, contract ending, etc., are all pretty innocuous. But don't tell them how you'd gotten fired for *xyz*. If you worked two weeks someplace before you had a breakdown in the office and were escorted out, leave that position off of your resume. They do not need to know any of this. A prospective employer can call the past one listed on your resume and ask, and there are no laws against them disclosing that you were fired. But, legally, a prospective employer does not *need* to know if you've ever had that sort of incident. Hopefully, you're catching on to what I'm saying.

3.) The only likely reason that they would want to know your past or current salary is to have a basis for the one that they'll offer. You want to make more? Good. Unless your past salary can be used to negotiate for more than what they're offering, then what you've made before is none of their business. Past pay is irrelevant to the current conversation. The person that they're talking with now has more experience and know-how, anyhow, and should be paid accordingly.

4.) Don't say who, specifically, your managers or coworkers are. Like I've said, this whole call could just be to pump for information, and you don't want to waste your time. If they seem less interested in you after you evade this kind of question, then that's a pretty good sign that they were trying to take you for a ride. Either way, there's no real reason that it would be beneficial to you to give this. Unless it's a calculated name-drop, don't talk about others.

And if they start asking for your mother's maiden name, your high school mascot, or maybe the three little numbers on the back of your credit card, just hang up. Sometimes it can be hard to tell the difference between a recruiter and a scam artist, but this is the clearest giveaway between the two.

WHEN YOU ANSWER

Now if the gig's description seems to more or less fit you

(although, like we've talked about, most of the time recruiters have no idea what they're really telling you), then by all means do your best to answer their questions concerning your experience and familiarity with the technologies that they had called about.

But before you answer their questions, I recommend that you ask a clarifying question before answering theirs. This way, you can answer the question as specifically as you can while also possibly gathering more information from their end. For example: if they ask you about Angular or some other JavaScript framework, then ask them *what* version they use and *how* they use it at the prospective company. If they want to know your experience with Azure, ask *how* they use it there, and then answer.

The recruiter might not fully understand what you're talking about, but knowing the specifics will help you to answer in a way that demonstrates your knowledge and potential value for that particular gig. You want them to know just how much they need you, after all. And, again, any and all information that you can get from them is going to prove to be of some value.

Also, did you happen to notice how I had framed those questions? The *what*, the *how*? Pay attention here, these are called "interrogative words". You start a question with an interrogative word and you are guaranteed to get something beyond a simple yes-or-no in return. This means that your question is "open-ended", and they have to respond with a solid fact or piece of information. This concept is the basis of Journalism 101 and the first day of interrogation training, but it is perfectly apt for this situation.

Let's review: you can use an interrogative word to ask an open-ended question and get more information than they had probably intended to give. Asking them a question that can be satisfied with a "yes" or "no" will often only get you that much. Spot the difference between:

"Is this job going to be in-office or remote?

versus

"Where would I be expected to do the work?"

One presents the only two options as in-office or remote, and this is usually the only response that you will get. The other phrasing, though, opens (excuse the pun) the possibilities up to whatever it is that the recruiter might know and say. They might answer in some roundabout way just to get to what's actually relevant. You might get to know all the different ways that exist for performing your duties. You might learn that they are more flexible than they wanted to appear. You might even be able to use this in negotiations. Either way, you get more out of it, and you want to get as much as possible.

Open-ended questions always start with an interrogative word, and an interrogative word is any one of what's known as the Five W's: *who, what, when, where,* and *why. How* is also included and can be used as well, although I guess it didn't really "flow" with the alliteration of the official list. Speaking of lists, here's one of the most basic open-ended questions that you can ask to get more information:

- "Why is the company trying to fill this role?"

Normally you would qualify this question with some context, like whether someone had quit or if there is simply more work than can be done by the current staff. Prefacing the question with either of these things are almost guaranteed not to give you anything more than a yes or a no. By keeping this question open-ended and not trying to essentially answer the question for them, they will probably tell you more than they otherwise would have.

- "What project or team are you hiring for?"

Again, vagueness is your friend here, and specificity kills.

- "Who would my manager be?"

You're going to need to really pay attention to what they say with this one. Be wary if they answer with a C-level title. It might seem impressive to be working right under the CEO, but this usually actually points to a poorly-managed company. Try to find out when the company started. It could also be that you're getting solicited by a very, very young company, and that could lead to some stability problems. Either way, it's very often not the grand idea that it appears to be. You might encounter some exceptional situation that I haven't, sure. But in the span of my (again, *long*) career, getting hired to work directly under a high-level title never worked out well. Take this all with respect to where you are in your career, though. If you're being hired for upper management, then it would make sense for you to be under the Big Guy. But if your title is something like a plain software developer, then it's a good bet that you're headed into a dysfunctional situation that you should probably avoid.

- "Where is the company headquartered?"

It's always a good idea to find out whether you're going to be working at the head office or some satellite office. Most of the time the caller won't tell you the company name, especially early on in the conversation. They're worried that you'll get off the phone and go apply independently if you know who wants you. This would cut them out of the deal entirely, and they'll obviously avoid that situation at all costs. Asking about the headquarters is an innocent way to get the information that could point to who it is that they're trying to hock you off to. Especially if it's a bigger company or with a well-known HQ, this could be the key to figuring out the company name earlier than they would want you to.

- "How soon does the hiring manager want to move on this position?"

This can be a good way to gauge their desperation for getting the role filled. You may even be able to get a backstory on the situation with the job. If you can get a sense of just how bad they want to get someone hired, this could prove to be good leverage in later negotiations.

- "How many people have you submitted to this role?"

This is another good gauging question. Knowing their need for a hire will help you to also know how far you can push the salary offer.

It's not hard to come up with your own, either. Start any question with a *who, what, why, when, where,* or *how,* and they're bound to deliver more information than they had really intended to.

And as I've already said, any information you can get is *good.* You should be doing every socially-acceptable thing that you can to get as much out of them as possible. Most of their power in the situation is derived from your ignorance. And with each question that you bother to ask, they lose that much more of what they have over you. Figure out how to use their answers to your advantage, and you may even find yourself in the upper hand.

CHAPTER SIX: THE INTERVIEW

TLDR:

- There are nuances to an IT tech interview that may not be anticipated by someone new in the field.
- Recruiters will often first have a "technical screening" that you will need to pass before they will set up an interview with the actual company. You can prepare by Googling the top 20 interview questions for your technology and practicing them.
- Research the company that you are interviewing with. Look up their current employees on LinkedIn to get an idea of the technologies they use, their turnover rate, etc.
- Dress professionally for the interview, but also take into account the company's overall attitude toward work/wear and tailor your outfit accordingly.
- Interview Theater #1: you need to ultimately

appear to be the smartest person in the room without drawing attention to it.

- Interview Theater #2: there could be a dynamic going on in the room that you have no part of. Your interviewer could be asking you inane, overly technical questions as a way to show off to somebody else.

- Beware and prepare for the potential egos of the nerds that you will often have to interact with during this process.

- The end of the interview is not the end of the interview.

FIRST THING FIRST

This isn't any sort of surprise, but you can't negotiate a rate for a job that you don't yet have. The order of things is that a recruiter calls you, you get the job, negotiate the rate, work. So, a recruiter calls you about a gig, and it sounds good. Good enough, even, to get into an interview. You get set up to meet with someone from the company and hopefully impress them enough to get the job.

Now, just how the Hell are you supposed to do that?

I'm supposing here that you are completely unfamiliar with the interview process. If you've got some number of years in the industry under your belt, you're probably safe to skip this chapter. This is aimed more toward IT newbies and the kids right out of college.

Because, surprisingly, there are quite a few of you. Some of you reading this may only have ever interviewed for your first job. You borrowed someone's blazer and pissed clean, and then started as a cashier the very next day. This is not going to be like that.

That's not to say that an interview is anything particularly nerve-wracking or impossible to pass. With the right prep work and some practice, you can get this thing down to a science and, inevitably, to success.

THE PREP WORK

The process of an IT tech interview has a few critical steps that you need to prepare for. Once the recruiter has an idea of how your resume fits their job opening, they will schedule an in-house cursory technical interview with one of their people. Sometimes they have you take a test, sometimes not. Most technical jobs will have a faux-technical ritual that they'll call a "technical screening" to see if you're worth getting in the door to the actual interview. Either way, they'll almost always have *something*.

What you need to do to get past this part of the process is to study up on the latest esoteric interview questions. Luckily, this is easily done. Use Google to find your technology's top 20 interview questions, then use these questions to refresh your memory. Practice. Assuming that you really are qualified for the job, then you will have little to no problem getting through this first screening.

After you get past that, the recruiter will then go ahead and set you up with the actual company. This is where things get slightly more difficult, but it's still not anything to truly stress over. There's just a few things that you need to do in the days between setting up your interview and when you finally walk into that room.

As soon as the recruiter confirms who the prospective company is, you need to start your research. Get a basic sense of their business. Look through their history. Check out their C-suite and senior managers. Find out the founder's dog's name, if you're feeling up to it. You just need to be learning everything possible so that you can demonstrate your knowledge and enthusiasm later on.

One key thing that you should absolutely look up are the company's current employees. Find their profiles through LinkedIn. You will be able to see about how long the employees have been there, which can help give you an idea about their turnover rate and potentially even how the workplace is. Most importantly, you'll also be able to get a sense of what kind of technologies that their employees are using, and ultimately what the company is hiring for.

Presentation, both in the appearance and personality, is key. What I call "interview theater" is this: you ultimately have to somehow appear to be the smartest person in the room without acknowledging or drawing attention to it. You may not have any acting experience, but this is the role that you need to play if you're looking to make the best impression on your interviewers.

Many actors attest that it's notably easier to "put on" the character when they get into costume. It's the same idea here when it comes to what you need to wear. Dressing correctly can do some surprising wonders in helping you to project that professional image in the interview.

You have to take into account *where* you're interviewing, however. For example, walking into a startup wearing anything like a suit is a great way to be seen as stuffy, while anything less than a custom-tailored suit at a Fortune 500 will get you written off for a poser. Different organizations have different office cultures, and the wardrobe expectations may vary. Again, this is why researching the prospective company is so important. Once you get a sense of the "vibe", for lack of a better term, of the company, then you can tailor your clothing to better fit with what other employees would be wearing.

But it's best to start with the basics: nothing sloppy, revealing, or baggy. That means nothing wrinkled, ripped, stained, etcetera. Your common sense will probably serve as a decent guide here. Dark-wash denim and a polo may be fine at some places, but we all know that your torn jeans and flip-flops would not do you any favors. What you ultimately want to strive for is something stylish but not overdone.

For most interviews, men will do fine in a suit jacket sans tie. For women, of course, it's a little bit trickier. Given the many options of women's workplace fashion, it's difficult to pinpoint any one standard outfit to go with. Again, the bottom line is to be stylish but not overdone. Any combination of a mid-length skirt/dressy pair of pants and a simple blouse or a conservative dress should be sufficient.

Now, your outfit is not the only visual detail that you need to pay attention to. If you're an actor in a costume, you still need to figure out the props that you'll be bringing onstage. The things that you take in with you convey just as much as the clothes that you choose to put on.

Any bags should be simple, sleek, and as clean-looking as your clothes. Phones should be silenced before you even step in the building. Have your ID on you and easily accessible, as you may need it for entrance at some offices. Always, always have something to write with and to write on. I've interviewed somewhere north of a thousand people throughout my career, and the only visual detail that I have ever negatively noticed was when they failed to bring something to write with and on.

You're likely to encounter at least one interviewer that *will* scrutinize each and every part of your appearance, though. There exists in our industry an entire nerd subculture that fixates on a weird, dressed-down ego, so it would do you some good to research your interrogators when possible and adjust accordingly. No matter who it is that interviews you, you need to take care not to come off in any way pretentious. For example, I'm a huge fan of Cavallini & Co., but do you think I'd ever bring one of their leather journals into an interview? No, because there is the off-chance that I'd look like a dick. Any pen, notebook, briefcase, glasses case, whatever that looks overly expensive or has a label should be left at home.

With all that in mind, your appearance is not what will ultimately get you the job. Like I've said, I've interviewed a lot of people in my life. Aside from the occasional jackasses that couldn't bother to bring a pen, I have never ever put stock into what someone was wearing or carrying with them. If you have the social and technical skills to get the job done, I'll decide to hire even if you came in dressed like the fucking Pagliacci clown. But, again, not all interviewers are going to take so little notice of what you show up in/with. What's going to ultimately matter the most is what you say and do during the interview to demonstrate yourself as the best candidate for the job, but how you visually present yourself usually ends up mattering much more than it should.

WHAT TO EXPECT/THE Technical Theater

I've probably already mentioned that I've worked at NASA (and before you roll your eyes, this is relevant but, even if it wasn't, don't try to tell me that you wouldn't brag about that fact forever). As everyone does, I was interviewed prior to getting offered the position. Who do you think I sat down with in that room? Some fellow tech person, a manager?

Try two supernerds with double PhDs each. Yes, *double*, as in two separate top-level degrees. They could sniff out a phony with nothing more than some classic CS and how an interviewee answered. Clearly, these guys were more than qualified to pick a candidate. But at the same time, they were continuously jumping to outdo each other with bullshit, arcane questions that had no real relevance to the interview. It didn't take long to realize that the interview was more about them than me.

That's another big part of the interview theater: there usually exists a dynamic that's got absolutely nothing to do with you. I've been on both sides of the interview for many years. In that time, I've noticed a strange phenomenon that flips the situation to something totally outside of your realm and relevance.

The commonly-understood (and logical) purpose of an interview is to meet with a candidate and weigh out their qualifications. What happens much too often, though, is that the person asking the technical questions becomes the one actually getting measured. This could be a real perception on their part, depending on who else is in the room. Remember, it will only rarely be just the two of you in there. There's typically a handful of other people to observe and ask questions. This will usually include at least one person with a title like "senior manager" that isn't as technical, but someone that others may look to impress with obscure tech talk. The technical interview could also just as likely be imagining this attention on them, or they could simply be a showoff. Nerds tend to fall in a strict pecking order, and a lot of them have a fragile sense of self-importance to boot.

I've seen this with nerds across the entirety of my career. I've often heard management say something along the lines of: "They're *smart*, but they're impossible to work with!" This is such a commonplace issue that I created a line graph to describe it.

The graph shows the correlation between IQ, a way to quantitively express someone's intelligence, and social skill, a more abstract concept that we assume is measurable here. As IQ rises, social skill tends to fall. Why?

Typically, a person with higher quantitative intelligence is going to be less able to communicate their ideas effectively and stay within social norms. This ranges anywhere from slight quirks to the complete eccentric. And as a lot of high-intelligence people are drawn into our industry, you are likely to come across this full spectrum more than most people ever will.

I've had to draw up this graph at every single organization I've ever worked at to explain to management that, basically, nerds are not like everyone else. The nerd elite tends to be terrible at communicating and getting along with others. Because of this, technical interview theater can get tricky, to say the least.

Their delicate little egos can often get in the way of making the right hiring decision. I have personally witnessed technically superior people get voted down because they posed a threat to some conceited nerd in the room. I've even seen women get voted down by one of those high-IQ sexists that couldn't stand the idea of a capable candidate also being female (note: misogyny is still rampant in STEM, but this is especially inexcusable). For the most part, these people are just trying to show off to the higher-ups in the room, and the interview becomes all about their own technical acumen rather than the personal actually being interviewed.

The only way to navigate this is to know when it's happening. Luckily, it's easy to tell when the interview has turned into a technical display by the kind of questions that they ask. A good giveaway is when they're grilling you with some really CS-type questions, like the difference between quicksort or bubble sort. And if it feels like one of the interviewers is trying to dominate you, then that's almost always what's going on. It's hard to say *what* you should do when it's happening, though. I have been both victim and bystander of this technical interview and unfortunately, it's not always enough to just know the answer.

The best thing that you can do to counter this kind of fuck-shit is to (gracefully) point it out. For example, that question about quicksort versus bubble sort? Mention that you haven't worked on bubble sorts since college. It's subtle, but you can probably call attention to the irrelevance of the question to even the people that have no idea what they're talking about, anyways.

One of my favorite answers is to write them off with: "When it comes to that, I normally just do a quick search on Google." I also like to explain how I could implement a couple different version of whatever the fuck they're asking you to see which one is the fastest. The best way that you can respond to these inane questions is to frame what they're looking for and how you would figure out the answer. That is usually as good, if not better, than actually *answering what they had asked.*

OTHER QUESTIONS

Not all questions are going to have this second intent. You're still going to have to deal with the regular checklist of questions that every other job asks. Obviously, you need to answer these as honestly and as best as you can, and hopefully make a good impression along the way. There's only two that we really need to talk about:

- "What would you say is your greatest weakness?"

Out of all of the (many) lame interview questions, this one has to be the lamest. It just *begs* for a disingenuous answer. Like seriously, do they think this'll get anybody to admit to their day-drinking or uncontrolled kleptomania here? My answer has always started with a little joke to acknowledge how stupid the question is. Something like: "You mean other than drinking 11 cups of coffee a day?" Say this with a light tone and pause for effect. It's easy to follow this up with the half-assed thing that they're probably looking for, like that you're a workaholic, or a perfectionist, or whatever. You get the idea.

- "Do you have any questions for me?"

This is actually a worthwhile question for both sides. For you, it's a last-minute chance to get any more information that you might need. For them, it can work as an indicator of your personality, as they'll see what information you might find valuable. The best questions that you can ask are the ones that prompt the interviewer to talk more about themselves and/or the company. For example:

1.) How long has everyone worked here/worked together?

2.) What type of SDLC does this office use, and when did you change over? How was the transformation?

3.) Who's been here the longest?

4.) What changes have you noticed since you started working here?

5.) What are your most and least favorite things about working here?

Another question that can help you stand out is to pick one thing mentioned by your interviewers and ask them for more information on that. It's a question tailored specifically to *that* interview, so that may help you stay in their mind later on.

AFTER THE INTERVIEW

So, you've survived the interrogation. You might already be

home, ready to make dinner and call it a day. You've done everything you can and all that's left is to wait for their call. It's out of your hands now, right?

Wrong.

You can take off that tie, but you're not done just yet. There's still a couple of things that you need to do to ensure that you're one of their top choices. We'll be talking about that in the next chapter.

CHAPTER SEVEN: THE FOLLOW-THROUGH

TLDR:

- The potential benefits of following up after an interview are obvious. However, most people don't actually do it.
- Being one of the few people to follow up can and often will be the deciding factor against all other candidates.
- The best way to follow up is to send a brief, handwritten letter to your interviewers.
- If you have poor handwriting and/or want to automate this task, there is a service that will write and send it for you.
- During the interview, ensure that you ask when they will be making their hiring decision. Call them then and check whether you got the job. Usually this will only confirm that you didn't, but this can occasionally lead to becoming their "second choice"

if/when their initial candidate ends up not accepting the job.

A SPORTS METAPHOR for Nerds

Let's go on a little tangent, for a minute, and talk about tennis. Or golf. Or archery. Baseball, even. I hope you're familiar with at least one of these or some other sport that requires you to hit something, and to hit it with some accuracy. Either way, you get the idea.

You step up with your racquet, bat, club, whatever. You've been taught how to square up and aim at the ball incoming through the air, or the one sitting on the tee. Shoulders straight and back, spine like a line, teeth gritted just so, all that. They show you how to hit. You hit. The ball goes. What do you do next?

You definitely *don't* just drop your equipment on the ground and walk away from it. The move isn't complete until your arms make a full swing and come back down. This, your instructor or coach or overzealous uncle tells you over and over, is called the follow-through. And the follow-through is just as important as the actual aim and strike. You have to finish with the follow-through.

I'd imagine that you're smart enough to get what I'm getting at here: what you do to ensure a follow-through after an interview can often make the difference between getting the job and getting ghosted. You're more than likely already aware of just how important this is, but it really can't be overstated: following up can and often will be what brings you to success.

HOW FOLLOWING up got me The Big Gig.

One last tangent, I promise. Let's go all the way back to 2001. It was early on in my career, and I'd just interviewed for something that looked to be a big project. They were creating a bill-drafting process for the Florida House of Representatives, and they needed someone like me on it. They'd already interviewed over ten people to find that one person. And if that one person like me turned out to actually *be* me, then I knew that this was the kind of high-profile gig that would launch me in the right direction.

I also knew that this gig wasn't going to be anything cushy. This would have me working as a "traveling consultant". Being billed as a traveling consultant meant that I would be facing an admittedly hellish workweek, as explained to me by the interviewer. It'd start on Sundays, when I would leave my home and then-girlfriend/now-wife to take a tiny commuter plane to Tallahassee. If you've never heard of Tallahassee, don't bother looking it up. If you've ever had to be in Tallahassee, I am so truly sorry. Once I had landed, I'd get to crash in a corporate apartment during the week and work out of the state capital (although, not to flex, but my office was two floors directly below the Governor's). I would work long days to make progress on the project until Thursday night, when I'd take that same horrible flight back home for the weekend. Rinse and repeat.

And repeat. And repeat.

Still, I wanted this job, and I wanted it *bad*. I knew that getting this on my resume would get me in the door to so many other, bigger opportunities. I decided that I just had to get this job, and so I did absolutely everything I could to get it. I walked into that interview prepared, prepped, primed, and ready to nail it as exactly the guy that they were looking for. I used all of my manners and gave them the very best answers that I could come up with. Call it conceited, but I was *good*.

That interview was pretty much the performance of a life-time. And you know what I did the minute I got out of it? I wrote and sent a letter to the two managers that were in there. Nothing too elaborate or ass-kissy. Just a quick thank-you. It took me maybe ten minutes to do, with the time it took to lick a stamp and seal the envelope included.

Those ten minutes were what put me ahead of all of the other candidates, and ultimately got me the job. I found out later on that those two managers had been suffering from a bit of what you can call "interview fatigue", or when every candidate starts to blend together. This often happens when companies fail to standardize the interview questions. In a situation where it was hard to remember anyone for anything and make the final decision, I was able to stand out with my follow-up and almost make their choice myself.

Which brings me to my whole point here. I was the only one out of those 10+ candidates to send a letter afterward. It's one of the most common pieces of workplace wisdom and yet, not many people actually enact a follow-through. I have trouble understanding *why* people wouldn't, since it's in no way difficult or time-consuming, but this lack is only going to make yours stand out that much more.

Because you never really know what is going on behind the scenes of a job prospect. You don't know what's going on even at the time of your interview, either. The person you're talking to may have gotten through fourteen other people that day, or they've got a headache, or their phone is going off under the desk. These unknown, seemingly unimportant variables really can and do come into play and take the interviewer's focus and attention away from you. You could be the absolutely perfect candidate, but if it's almost lunchtime and they can only think about that meatball sandwich they've got waiting in the break room, then you might not stand out for what you are.

And of course, you want to stand out in all the best ways. Do you really think it'd be safe or smart to just trust that they're going to remember you? If you are going to max out your chances of getting the gig, then you need to do everything that you can. Following up after an interview is one of the easiest and most efficient ways of boosting yourself to the top of their candidate list.

HOW TO FOLLOW Through

There are two essential things that you need to do after you interview for a gig. If the place was on fire and you hated every second of it, then there obviously won't be anything to do after. So, we're going to go ahead and assume that you only saw green flags in the interview and want the job. Here are your next steps:

The very first thing you should do when you get home from that interview is write and send a handwritten thank-you note to the hiring manager and/or the person that conducted your interview. Yes, I said *handwritten*. That's the kind of old-fashioned tactic that works best to convey a sense of sincerity from your end. An email just isn't going to cut it here. Now, I happen to have the handwriting similar to that of a dyslexic Australian labradoodle. If you write in a similarly illegible fashion, I highly recommend using a service called Handwrytten. All you have to do is type out the message and choose a handwriting style, and they'll use robots to write out and send your letter. Those of us who are somehow competent with a pen and paper may still want to check it out, as this service will semi-automate the process of following up. Our type always looks for efficiency, after all.

Whatever way that you choose to get this part done, you have to ensure that it's done *correctly* and *timely*. Sending it to the wrong place or sending it too late will completely negate any possible influence that the letter may have had. Make sure that you get the right address before you even leave the interview, as the place where you interviewed is often not listed as the actual main address. Then, once you get home, write and send it to that address. I already said to do it the minute that you get home, and I'll take up the page space to say it again: you need to write and send that letter right when you get home from the interview. Every minute that ticks by is another minute that they might be making their hiring decisions, and you want to get back in their mind as soon as the postal service will permit. They need to receive your letter within three days after your interview for it to really matter. So, yeah, you want to get that letter on the way as quickly as you can.

If you want to really make sure that they remember you (which, again, you *should*), I would try to think of something that happened or was said in your interview that you can mention in the letter. That way, they can definitively connect the name on the card to the face in the room, and the chances of your resume coming back up for them are all the better. What you mention should be something small but memorable. For example, say they comment on your tie/article of clothing. That would make for a very easy thing to remind them of in the letter. It wouldn't necessarily be too far to even craft some small, specific thing to wear or say in the interview so that you can later mention it in the letter. This, though, would obviously need to be well-integrated and not appear as an overtly conspicuous choice. This is a calculated action, so if you make what you're doing obvious, then you're just going to come off as some kind of creepy Patrick Bateman cosplayer.

Not sure what to write? It's not hard to imagine that you're reading this as a twenty-something that's never written an actual letter. That's pretty understandable. I mean, the younger generation has never really had to. Or you could just be stuck on what to say. Either way, you could start by more-or-less copying my template. Tweak as needed, of course.

Dear [NAME OF PERSON THAT YOU INTER-VIEWED WITH],

Thank you for taking the time to interview me on [WEEK-DAY, MONTH AND DATE]. I really admire your organiza-tion, and I hope that I was able to convince you that I can help your teams to reach your goals. [MENTION SPECIFIC DETAIL THAT CAN REMIND THEM OF WHO YOU ARE]. If you have any further questions, please don't hesitate to contact me at [EMAIL ADDRESS AND PHONE NUMBER].

Sincerely,

[YOUR NAME]

As you can see, it's not particularly lengthy or detailed. I'm not going on for paragraphs about how much I love them or all of the things that I could do for them. You can go ahead and save that suck-up shit for someone else. The key here is simple, short, and sincere. They'll understand and appreciate the gesture much more if it all fits comfortably on one page.

The second thing that you need to do is something that you need to actually start before the letter. Before you shake their hand and exit the interview, absolutely do not forget to ask when they will be making their decision. Remember that approximate date, and then pay them a phone call.

Usually, the interviewer is going to be the one to prompt this. You know how at the end, most of the time, their final question is: "Do you have any questions for me?". Ask them then. It not only demonstrates that you truly care about the outcome of this interview, but it's also the most socially graceful time for you to get your answer.

If that fateful decision day has come and passed without any word from them, it's safe to assume that you didn't make the cut. Still, there's no harm in following up with a quick phone call. They can't fault you for making sure that you didn't get the job. And that's what you're doing, just making sure, because you never really know. Maybe your call could be coming right after their first choice ended up declining. Worst case scenario is that you're going to affirm their "no", and we all know that rejection is a part of the process.

On that word "no": it goes both ways. You are free and able to reject a job just as much as a job is to reject you. In fact, you probably should be rejecting more offers than you are right now. Have you ever jumped at a job only to find that all that glitters isn't gold? Learning the merits of and how to use "no" can save you from a lifetime of future regrets.

CHAPTER EIGHT: LEARN TO SAY "NO"

TLDR:

- You need to examine each and every job opportunity with a critical eye.
- Recruiters are not looking to place you in the best opportunity or even the job most suited to your skillset. They will put you wherever they can so that they can be done and get to the next.
- There are a pretty clear set of red flags to watch out for when dealing with a recruiter and/or interviewing for the job. If you spot any, it's more than likely best to decline the position.
- The promise of a high rate can often get us to overlook aspects of a job that we would consider a "red flag" if less money was involved.
- You have to consider any gig as a potential dead-end for your career due to how quickly technologies change and/or become obsolete.
- Job postings in our industry can and often will be

essentially "mislabeled" due to the recruiters/HR/higher manager/etcetera not fully understanding what they really need to hire for.

- Asking a few questions to clarify the job's day-to-day and responsibilities will often be enough to figure out what the job would actually entail.
- Ultimately, trust your instinct. If you think that something stinks, that's because it does.

THE NEED OF "NO"

"No" can be hard for some to say. A lot of people want to seek out new opportunities, and that two-letter word can seem counterintuitive to doing that. However, you have to remember that the grass is not always greener on the other side. It's actually just as important to know when and how to pass on bad gigs as it is to jump at the right ones.

Another key is being able to tell if the recruiter doesn't actually know who they are looking for. Luckily, this is usually easy to spot as soon as even that first phone call. Pay attention to the words that they're using when describing the job. If it sounds like some technical nonsense, that's because it is. They don't really know who it is that they're trying to get, and you will end up wasting time in an interview for a job that you don't want or can't do.

Above all, your time is invaluable. Let's keep it from being wasted.

WHY/WHEN to Say No

When on the search for the next gig, we often overlook certain details that seem somewhat insignificant in the moment, but inevitably end up being more substantial than we could've ever imagined. The somewhat standoffish manager in the interview turns into a raging asshole on the job; never getting a clear answer about the insurance means you're now having to drop a considerable portion of your paycheck just for healthcare. Ignoring these little things that don't sit right with us will only grow into a bigger problem later, and we ultimately end up settling at something less than we wanted or what we even deserve.

When a recruiter first calls you about the possibility of a next gig, they're only trying to establish a few quick things:

1.) Do you seem, from that first cursory screening, able to do the job?

2.) Will you do this job at the rate that they are paying (or possibly even less)?

3.) Do you have any deal-killing personality flaws that they can detect over the phone?

And that's it. And if you seem like you pass this first brief scan, then into the pile you go. The most optimistic idea of a recruiter is that they work to get the best fit of the best person into the best job. Well, we all know that that rarely (if ever) is the recruiter's real objective. They're trying to put people into jobs, regardless of whether that's actually the right person going into the right job. They don't give a shit about proper placement. They do what they think they need to do to get things done. Sometimes that even means that they might try fitting a square block into a triangular hole.

Unfortunately, you're looking at dealing with many, many of these kinds of recruiters throughout your career. What they'll do for you, at best, is waste your time. If you don't proceed with the caution and thorough thought that I've advised, you could potentially fall into their trap of a terrible and/or misplaced gig.

The bright side of it is that they get a lot easier to spot with experience. Of course, you're not going to have any if you're fresh out of college or fresh into the field. But, clearly, I've got some. Over the years, I've noticed a list of pretty consistent red flags that pop up during the course of what turn out to be/should have been "no" gigs. Any one of these should tell you that it's probably best to turn the job down.

Red Flags:

1.) No technical interviewer. If you've made it this far and the recruiter never pulls in a technical interviewer, then they're just throwing resumes against the wall.

2.) A vague job description, especially one that doesn't list any specific technologies.

3.) An overly broad or incorrect job title.

4.) Always ask: is this a new position, or are you replacing someone? You could just be the next sucker that they're trying to rope in after the last guy walked out (and usually while leaving a mess behind).

5.) Multiple calls from multiple recruiters for the same position.

6.) Lack of follow-up. You should always be kept in the loop.

7.) Lack of candor. If it feels like they're trying to hide something, they are.

This is by no means a complete list. This is only a good catch-all for most of what's out there. There likely exists situations that are shady and slimy in their own uniquely terrible way. You might even start noticing other things that feel "off" throughout the course of your dealings with recruiters. Note those down too. It's not right that we need to keep our guard up over employment prospects, but it's better than getting conned into a situation that we quite literally did not sign up for.

· · ·

WHY TO BE WARY OF "YES"

The thing about saying "yes" to something also means saying "no" to all of the other possibilities presented at that time. One or any of those "no's" could have been the better opportunity. Or maybe they all were, and you later find that you'd jumped to take what turned out to be the absolute worst pick of the bunch.

The promise of a big paycheck tends to make people forgive other aspects that may have gotten more thought if less money was involved. Like, if you're on a date with a model, you may be more likely to ignore the fact that they brought their knife collection with them. In both cases, you're probably going to learn that all that glitters isn't really gold. Sometimes, the rate isn't going to be the most important part of it.

Selling yourself to the highest bidder, regardless of the project involved, is a great way to get yourself in a career pickle. For example: even if you've been using a certain technology for five years, people will still hesitate to hire you if you didn't use it in your last project. Each and every gig must be considered as a potential dead end. The most ideal gig would be a project that uses the newest version of a technology. A perfect example of this is Angular 1 and Angular 2. One version over the other, and your skills literally are no longer applicable.

But you don't have to necessarily sit and agonize over your choices. The difference between taking a shit gig and a good one could really just mean stepping back for a second and asking yourself a few questions.

1.) Is this a greenfield gig or a brown one? As in, are you going to be fixing someone else's bullshit, or are you going to be able to create your own?

2.) Consider project longevity. Any chance that they're trying to hide the fact that the gig is a super short-term project and you're out the moment it's done?

3.) Think about the benefits. Does the 401k vest only after your project is basically over? You really have to watch for this. It's shocking how often they try to pull this nasty little trick. And what about everything else? How quickly do the benefits kick in? Do you have to wait 30 days? 60 days? How expensive are they? Will the company cover them? Even a portion of them? And what about for your family?

4.) Did you notice any other red flags when you went in for the interview: an air of fear about the office, no comradery among co-workers, low working morale, high turnover, unclear job description, no or vague explanation as to why the role is open, anything else?

The old adage to "go with your gut" is also perfectly applicable here, too. Asking these questions may better help inform your decision, but consulting your own intuition is just as valuable. If you take a sniff at the air and think that something stinks, that's because it does. Period.

But if the potential gig passes all the checks and seems right by you, then congratulations! You've probably found a good gig. We'll talk about how to negotiate for an even better rate for it in the next chapter.

THE ACCURACY ISSUE

It goes without saying, but sometimes people don't exactly do their jobs. It could be as little as neglecting to take out the trash while closing up shop, or as catastrophic as the careless captain that ended up sinking an entire cruise ship. Why that matters is where it becomes specifically our problem. That is, when the people in charge of accurately describing a job fail to accurately describe a job. And it happens in our industry more than you might expect. The result of this is essentially some "mislabeled" results that come up when we're searching for the next gig. This means that we unfortunately have to waste our own time to weed them out, or risk getting stuck somewhere that we don't belong.

You can start by asking yourself what exactly it is that the company needs. The job title may say "web developer", but there could be a chance that they actually mean "designer" or "architect". A lot of the time, HR assigns a job title that bears absolutely no similarity to what you'd actually be doing. Needless to say, it's important that you take it upon yourself to find out what your specific day-to-day responsibilities would be. If the actual expectations of the job don't align with the posted ones, then that makes for a red flag.

If the direct manager is absent from the interview or if they can't verbalize exactly what you will be doing, then that makes for the absolute mother of all red flags. Unless you're intuitively colorblind, this should be getting you to seriously reconsider the job.

Sometimes this positional vagueness is intentional. If, for example, the company is a Fortune 500-sized organization, then the title may only be assigned as it is so that they can get more money for the position, as they've been having a hard time filling it as-is. This is how web developers get architect titles. Don't let them just throw you anywhere. Their bureaucratic reasoning or pure mismanagement does not trump your career.

For the most part, red flags are not too difficult to see. For the most part, the biggest ones will be waving themselves right in your face. You'll eventually get pretty good at spotting them from miles away. But if you go into this with rose-colored glasses, you're going to end up losing. I promise.

CHAPTER NINE: LET'S MAKE A DEAL

TLDR:

- You need to know the current market rate for a prospective job before going into negotiations. Do not consult the salary estimators online, as those numbers are almost always bullshit. Use LinkedIn and/or ask around on relevant subreddits and real-life colleagues to get the most accurate idea of the going rates.
- Avoid making the first offer. That first number acts as an "anchoring principle" that dictates how the rest of the negotiation will go.
- When you go first, your number will become the absolute maximum that you can get. When they go first, their number will become the absolute minimum.
- If you are forced to make the first offer, respond with a range. Put the rate that you are actually looking for on the low end of this range.

- Don't ever accept their first offer. Always try to make a counter-offer.
- Use information that you've gathered about the job to push for more. The long commute, the bad insurance, etcetera, all work as solid arguments for a higher rate.
- The one and only time that you should make the first offer is when you are dealing with an HR department. HR is given set pay parameters from their higher-ups, so you need to tell them as early as possible that you could possibly be their exception.
- You will never get more if you don't ask for it. Period.

DOWN TO THE Deal

Alright, you've made it this far. You've gotten all the way to the table, they want you, and it's all coming down to the hard numbers. And even here, they may still try to fuck you over.

What they are going to try to do is push you to make the first offer. What you are going to try to do is keep your mouth shut. Any number that flies out is only going to keep you from any possible higher one. This chapter will help you get the best rate possible, and to get it from the other side.

SET YOUR PRICE

Knowledge is power. We all know that. When it comes to negotiation, your opponent's biggest advantage is your own ignorance. They could be offering you, say, a $50k annual for a position. That number might seem relatively all right in the moment, but what if you found out that the average pay is more like $90k? You could be getting seriously screwed without even knowing it, because you didn't *know* in the first place.

Have you ever stopped to consider why it's seen as crass or distasteful to talk about salaries in corporate culture? If you learned that someone in the same position was making more, then it'd be more than reasonable to ask for comparable pay. They know this, and that's why they don't want you to.

You need to get a good idea of the market price before you even get into the interview. The importance of understanding the going rates cannot be overstated. You need to get a good assessment and evaluation of what someone with your experience, skills, title, etc., should expect to get.

Aside from saving yourself from getting fucked, knowing the going rates can also save you from looking like an asshole. Asking for too little (or even too much) can absolutely ruin your chances of negotiating a fair compensation. For example: you ask for $65/hour when the going rate is $100/hour, and you seriously lose out on pay. But you ask for $100/hour when the going rate is $65/hour, and you're going to come off as an idiot who couldn't even bother to research the market and not even seem worth the time it'd take to consider you. The end result here is that the recruiter will pretty quickly cross you off of their list of potentials, but the real danger is that you may even be burning a bridge to not just that one recruiter, but to the entire company. And when the industry is as tight as it can be, you really don't want to be going around pissing people off like that.

So, you need to do your homework. There's a couple different ways that you can go about figuring what the market rate is. One of the most seemingly obvious methods would be to jump to the Internet. Before you do, don't. I can tell you with confidence that those online salary surveys and rate estimators are not at all accurate. I have no idea where these people are getting their numbers from, but they always seem to be off by anywhere between 15% to 20% from the actual rate. And this margin of error is never in your favor.

What sucks most about this is that these are the same inaccurate sources that companies get their salary expectations from, which just makes everyone's job that much harder. Going off of these inaccurate rates makes everyone, the hiring and the potential hires included, seem unreasonable. I won't go on a tangent about my tinfoil-hat theory as to why these numbers are so off, but I have my suspicions that they could be extrapolating missing data from cities that have more respondents. I mean, how else could any of these organizations have an opinion on salaries in smaller cities? Anyways, it's Big Conspiracy and not really worth our time. The point here is to *never* consult these sources to base your worth, unless you want to be worth less.

That's not to say that the Internet isn't going to be a good way to get accurate rate info. You can find a gold mine of valuable info if you know where to look, and if you know how to sort through all of the misinformation first. The very first thing you should do, though, is to contact everyone you know in the industry. Real-life colleagues can always produce some valuable and relevant information.

Next, you should post across a couple of subreddits. If I need to explain Reddit to you, then you may need to take a break from this book and go check out www.reddit.com. If you somehow get nothing else from this book, you will at least get to discover your new favorite website. If you are otherwise familiar (or, as a lot of our crowd are, *very* familiar) with it, I've listed a couple subreddits below where you can post your salary questions. Be sure to mention your experience, if any, and the city that you are looking in. In my experience, I've found that a lot of other posters are typically going to be pretty helpful and their information is generally good. However, as with anything you get on the Internet, be sure to keep your Bullshit Detector just lightly on while reading comment threads.

A couple good subreddits:

r/cscareerquestions

r/ITCareerQuestions

r/programming

These three are just the most broad and popular places to get you started. If somehow none of these subs deliver on any good comments, it's a safe bet that there are even more subreddits to try posting on. You could always dig through another user's comment or post history to try to find any other relevant subreddits. It might feel a little invasive, but you can generally find somewhere new by doing this. Either way, you are generally going to get a pretty good return of information for the relatively minimal amount of time that it takes to type up a question.

LinkedIn still exists, of course. You can always poke around their job search area and find a couple of jobs in your field of expertise with the salary/rate info. This can give you a pretty good idea of what other people are getting offered to build your basis for what you should be paid.

LOSERS GO FIRST

I don't know if you've ever happened to have seen *The Wolf of Wall Street*, but it's fantastic and has almost nothing to do with what we're talking about here. Leonardo DiCaprio wears nice suits and rips people off. Sounds a bit like some recruiters, but that's about it.

I say "about" because there's one scene that makes perfect sense here: Leo's character is trying to get some idiot over the phone to buy bad stocks. He talks and talks, and then he stops.

And then he waits. And in a voiceover, he lets the audience know:

"Whoever speaks first loses."

There, he's trying to get some poor sucker to buy worthless stock. Here, you're just trying to keep from being some poor sucker that gets cheated out of a fair pay. This rule applies to both sides: whoever speaks first loses. Except in one very particular circumstance that I will detail later, you want to do everything you can to not make the first offer.

The most basic premise of a negotiation goes more or less like this. You, the holder of the value, want to sell for as high as you can. Them, the seekers of the value, want to buy for as low as they can. You start up, they start down, and eventually you both meet somewhere in the middle.

When it comes to negotiating with recruiters and/or HR, these lines are no longer so simple. Again, you hold the value—yet it seems that they're the ones with the power in these sit-downs. They have professional training in how to get you for as little as possible. You probably get uncomfortable pointing out a problem with your food at restaurants. Their training is compounded by practice in actual negotiations maybe even every *day*. You will do this maybe a couple times in your entire life. This is not the cut-and-clear way of haggling seen in markets or used-car lots.

When you make the first offer, you now have the rest of the negotiations set at or even lower than that number. Yes, even lower. The best case here is that they'll meet your rate and everyone goes home happy. Almost invariably, though, they are going to make a counter offer. That counter offer is always going to be lower. End of story.

Now when they make the first offer, the converse is true. You are now granted the ability to either accept their offer (which, don't) or to counter with something higher. When you say a number, it's unlikely that you'll actually get it, and just about impossible to get anything higher. When they say a number, that's kind of like setting the "absolute minimum". They'd have to be really, really slick (and you've have to be really, really stupid) to get you for any lower than that. Once you know the very minimum that they're willing to pay, then you know you're in a good place.

I'm not just talking out of my ass here. There is real science that you can study to back up everything I've learned out on the field. If you're more of a math person, go ahead and check out the Rubinstein bargaining model. The hypothetical situation it proposes is over two people bargaining over a share of a pie, and gives a quantified formula to express how the first offer influences all subsequent ones.

Or, if that's all a bit over your head, there's a pretty succinct article on the research done by Northwestern Kellogg. In "Negotiation tips: Who's on first?", Professor Leigh Thompson explains how the first offer acts as an anchoring principle that will dictate the rest of the negotiation and the ultimate outcome.

If it helps to visualize, think of the anchoring principle as exactly that— an anchor. This first number hooks and holds any further offers because it creates a cognitive bias for your opponent. You've said this one, and now they're going to use it to base any further and/or final offers. The research had pointed to a strong correlation between that initial offer and the one that both parties ended up agreeing on. I have observed this anchoring principle play out over and over in exact throughout my entire adult life. It's real, and it really will come back to bite you if you decide to try ignoring the science.

That being said, it's oftentimes a bit difficult to get the recruiter to give you a number. Like I've said, they're not the unpracticed dope that they're hoping you to be. They know all the plays, and they only ever want to keep you at the disadvantage. So a lot of the time, they'll refuse to move forward without some number on your end. This doesn't mean that you're necessarily forced out of the upper hand here, though. And you don't need to lock up with them in some kind of Western showdown. You just need to answer with a range. Make the low end of that range the actual number that you would accept. The mid to high range, well, then you've still opened the door to a rate that you'd walk out *very* happy with.

AND LOSERS TAKE the First Offer

Hopefully, you remember all the way back to Chapter 5? I wasn't telling you to ask all those questions and do all that research just for shits and gigs (well, for *actual* gigs, but anyways). At this point in the process, all the information that you've gathered has now sharpened into a weapon that you can use to negotiate for a number higher than they've put on the table.

By now, you should have a good understanding of the actual scope of this job and know the rate that you would be willing to take for it. You've done all of your homework, and you're coming to the table as well-informed and as prepared as you can be. Let's say you manage to get them to make the first offer. And let's say that offer is exactly at your number, or even above it. Do you congratulate yourself on immediately getting what you want, take it, and go home happy?

No.

The first offer is never going to be the highest. Again, the whole goal here is to get as much as you can. The single best thing you can do to maximize your chances of getting more is to never take the first offer, and to never shy away from rejecting it with a reasonable counteroffer.

Refer back to all of the answers that you had collected. Any one of these answers can be picked up and thrown back at them to counter an offer. You don't even have to be an ass about it, either. A couple examples of how to do it tactfully:

- They say they want to offer you $43 an hour. You know that you have to work in the office. You've looked it up, and this place is nowhere near your house. You know that this job would mean a long commute. You (politely!) inform them that you will have to sit in the car for two hours each day for the job, and so somewhere around $48 to $50 an hour would make you comfortable. If you have to spend more time out of your day just in pursuit of the work, then the rate should be adjusted accordingly.
- They come in at the exact rate that you were hoping for. But you know that their insurance is a little more expensive than average, and you let them know. $5 to $10 more per hour, you say, is what you are looking for. On account of the insurance.

Doesn't it just sound so much better when you put it this way? More reasonable, more confident? When your counter-offer is prefaced with a specific *why*, it makes it a bit more difficult for them to say no.

It's nerve-wracking, I know. Most of us in the IT crowd are pretty averse to conflict, and this really does feel like a conflict. You have to keep your words steady and push down the idea that you somehow shouldn't be *allowed* to ask for what you want, or even for more.

It's taken me years and years to get over the fear that if I asked for more, then the first offer would somehow get rescinded. Like, for some reason they'd be so offended by the audacity that I'd dare ask for more than their "generous" offer that they would just up and decide that then I shouldn't even get that much. The general human nature worries over possible loss.

There's even a term for it: *loss aversion*. When negotiating, especially when there is some sense of a deadline to reach an agreement, we may often find ourselves driven more by the fear of losing the current offer than by the desire to reach a better one. There's a pretty masterful book on negotiations, *Never Split the Difference* by Chris Voss, that details this condition much more in-depth than I can here. As an aside, his book should be considered essential reading for anyone trying to get anything out of anybody. That, of course, includes you.

Chris Voss explains how loss aversion works in action during a ransom negotiation with kidnappers. Now obviously, that's not anywhere near to what's happening here. You're not trying to bargain for your grandmother's life—you're working out a rate that you can live on. The only real similarity is that you are going against someone much more experienced and cutthroat in negotiations than you could ever be, and they know that. And they're looking to prey on your inexperience and anxieties in coming to the table to get you to agree to a number far lower than you should.

I'd liken the nervousness in negotiation to what we'd all feel as kids when we'd try getting a date (or maybe you're still playing the pool, good for you). All these insane hypotheticals flashed through your head as you got closer to the question. Did any of them actually become reality? The worst that probably happened was just "no" and then avoiding them for a little while. Maybe some minor embarrassment, a bruised ego. But we've all pushed through this possibility of rejection for the possibility of going out with someone (or even "the one", if you're a little sappy like that). The same way that we've swallowed our fear here is the same way that you can do it to hold yourself at the negotiations table.

I can promise you that nothing catastrophic is going to happen if you counter them. They're not going to jump over the desk and bite your head off. They won't scream and send you out of the building. As long as you are sincere and polite when you make your counters, the absolute worst thing that can or will occur is that they'll say no.

"No" is totally fine. "No" just means that they won't go any higher than the current offer, or that they'll only meet you at the first offer (which should be something you wanted, anyway). If they won't budge on a low rate and you end up walking, then you wouldn't want to work there anyway.

The biggest thing to keep in mind when you're in negotiation is that if you don't try countering their offer, then you won't be able to get a higher rate. It's as simple as that. If you don't ask for more, then you will never get more. Ever.

THE ONE EXCEPTION: HR

We have yet to really discuss how to handle doing business with an HR department. This is because, for the most part, you'll have to be going through a recruiter. But also, for the most part, almost everything that we have talked about is applicable to them as well. Not quite *everything*, though. There's a section here because HR is the one exception to everything I've said in this chapter so far.

Okay, so only losers give away their number first, unless it's with HR.

This is the one time that it'll be preferable to set your price first. And I mean *first*, like probably before you even have all the facts. Because an HR department at a large company works and thinks a bit differently than a recruiter. Gladys the HR rep is not going to have a dog in this fight the way that Rip-Off Rick the Recruiter does. HR only sees the parameters given by the company. Of course, everything is always negotiable, but they don't care. Their objective is to find someone with the needed skill set at a particular price, and thinking anywhere outside of that box is not normally their strong suit.

Here's how it will usually go with them. They'll tell you very early on that the job pays only x or y. Now as soon as they say that, you need to ask them whether or not they would be willing to pay more for the right candidate. It might take some pushing to get an actual answer out of them. You can nudge them a bit by giving them facts like salary surveys. Polite persistence is what you're aiming for here. Show them that you've done your homework and you won't take a "no" all that easy.

What you ultimately want out of them is a (perhaps begrudging) "yes". You want to hear that, if the situation called for it, they would possibly entertain a higher right for the right person. As soon as you get that, then you need to jump on explaining and justifying why it is that you want more than what they are currently offering. You have to build them a case that's both careful and concise. The second that you step out of their given parameters, they are going to shut you down by simply saying that the job will not pay that.

These given parameters can almost always be expected for an HR at a large company. In fact, Fortune 500 companies are especially infamous for this. Their rigidity with their (often pretty low) rates is an in-house rule that keeps their profit margins up. It also keeps the real talent from bothering to apply and is probably part of the reason that recruiters came to exist in the first place.

So, an HR department and a recruiter are both doing their best to get you at a lower rate (as they are paid to do). The real difference between an HR department and a recruiter is that they both have their own *special* reasons for doing it. A recruiter wants to personally make as much money as possible, especially at your expense. HR is only going by their higher-up's rules and their own lack of imagination. But if you flag yourself early on that you might be the exception to the prescribed parameters, then you might be able to find some flexibility.

With HR, you don't get to wait to gather information the way that you need to with recruiters. You can drag it out with recruiters until you have enough to build a solid argument for more, but that's just not so with HR. What you need to do is make a case, right in the moment, that's good enough for them to pitch it to management. And you really, really have to watch how you say things here. If they hear even a hint of arrogance or ego from you about the current rate, you're done.

The two things that can happen in this situation are either that HR holds on their rate, or they will go ahead and pitch your case to management. If they get management to agree, you could probably get away with something like a 15-20% increase in a supposedly set rate. But if they won't or "can't", then that's just the end of the fight.

If you're looking to maximize your earnings, you can't just accept whatever number they try to give you. The worst thing that happens if you challenge them is that they'll hold firm on their offer, and that's it. The best thing that could happen is, well, *more*. How much more, no one can really say, but you won't get to find out if you don't try.

Above all, you have to ask for it.

CHAPTER TEN: ALWAYS BE IMPROVING

TLDR:

- You are the prize, but you have to show that to prospective employers/clients if you expect to be treated and paid as such.
- Your personal "brand" refers to what others can find and see about you.
- At the very least, you need to control the immediate results of Googling your name.
- Creating a social media presence that projects an image of expertise and professionalism will put you above other candidates.
- The two best ways to go about establishing this presence is to keep up a blog with relevant content and/or create a social media platform to engage with others on your areas of expertise. Either will work, but both are recommended.
- Anything that you ever put on the Internet can and will come back around to affect your

life/career. This includes even the supposedly "private" posts.

- Your skillset can quickly become obsolete if you don't stay up-to-date on the current technologies used in the industry.
- The easiest way to find out the current technologies is to look at the requirements and experience listed in job postings.
- If you don't know something, learn it. If you already know something, learn it better. You always have room for improvement.

THE PRIZE

Any chance you remember what I said earlier? And I mean way earlier, like at the very start of the book? It's ok if not. I'm not even going to make you go back to the second sentence of the fourth paragraph in the foreword, because I'll say it again:

You are the prize. Yes, you, sitting there with the paperback or tablet. You have dedicated your life to learning the ins and outs of IT. Most people can't even manage to put a Safe Filter on their kid's browser. Computers and companies depend on the people who can make technology go, and you can make technology go. You're not just some warm body looking to push paper or stand in a store. Your skillset is specific and vital to an increasingly important part of how our society functions, and it's only going to grow. We really might all end up with those Apple implants or straight-up cyborgs as the next step in evolution. Who do you think is going to be called to program and manage the systems behind all this?

You are the prize. But until you truly accept this fact and start acting accordingly, nobody is going to treat you for your full worth. Recruiters will fuck you over a barrel if they think it'll get them an extra penny; companies will try to get you for as close to nothing as they can. Your modesty and sense of wanting to be "agreeable" with their insulting offers is only helping them increase their profit margins. This all comes at the cost of your ability to live comfortably, to live how you deserve. You are the prize, and yet you let yourself act gracious under the boot of their greed. Stop.

The good news is that it's easy to get out of this and to start showing your real value. Here we'll be detailing how to build your very own personal brand, and how to make yourself the most desirable asset that you can be. This chapter could (and maybe should) be a book in it of itself, but I'll give you the best run-down that I can.

YOUR FIRST STEP

While hopefully avoiding any egocentrism, here's what I want you to do right now: look me up. That's Scott, with two t's, Turman. Type that into Google. Check the first page of results. What do you see?

What you're going to find is *my* Twitter, Facebook, LinkedIn, and website (that's www.scottturman.com). You're not going to see me tagged in any less-than-flattering photos or the mugshot of another Scott Turman. I have gotten hold of and completely control the immediate results for my name. When a client or prospective employer looks me up, they only see what I want them to see, and that information presented to them is what hopefully compels them to trust me/my brand.

Yes, brand. You are your very own brand too, ever since you entered the workforce with a blank resume and on minimum wage. In capitalism, you either make money through providing products or a service. You provide a service so, essentially, you sell yourself. That's your brand. Do you have any idea what your brand advertises to others?

Go ahead and search yourself. What do you—and anyone else that Googles your name—see? Are you drunk off your ass in pics that you shouldn't have put up? Have you posted any lengthy political rants on a public profile? Do you happen to share your name with a prolific adult film star? Any of these could shoot your chances of a job dead in the water. Don't believe supposed policies or even the law about respecting the privacy of your personal life. Companies *will* look you up, and they definitely *won't* hire you if you've got absolutely anything out there that could potentially bring harm to their business.

Your brand starts with your voice and ends with your reach (either real or perceived). That said, you need to start your brand by picking a platform. You can do this either with a blog or on any social media outlet where you can acquire a following. You need to be active on this platform and update it regularly with content to solidify and strengthen your image as a professional. When a contact, client, or employer sees this platform, you want them to see someone who can do the job well and will be pleasant to work with. At the very least, you don't want them to see someone who doesn't know what they're doing or someone who is going to make problems for HR.

Of course, this is ultimately an ideal image that you project for the professional world. I'm not saying to necessarily suppress yourself by holding back on the gym selfies and not fighting with your cousin in the comment section of a news article. If you choose to conduct yourself online in a way that differs from what I've advised, that's entirely your decision. But if you're going to do it, do it *privately*. Keep personal accounts separate from your professional ones, and keep those closed only to friends/followers. If a random profile requests to follow any of your personal accounts, don't approve it. It's incredibly sneaky and usually even illegal, but there always stands a pretty good chance that it's a fake account set up by a company to snoop on potential employees. Yes, they really do try this. If you don't have at least one mutual, it's best to be safe and block them. You really can't be too cautious with this, especially if you decide to have some potentially compromising content on the Internet.

Just one more note about that: I know I sound like some afterschool special, but you really do need to understand that anything and everything you put on the Internet really is for forever. An off-color comment you made on Facebook in 2012 could come back and get you fired *today*; that revealing pic you posted on your supposedly "private" Snapchat story could cost you job opportunities for the rest of your life. Nobody wants to hire or work with someone that could cause them problems because of their personal life. Don't let your personal life be a problem. It's your freedom of speech, sure, but is a post really worth your livelihood?

THE CARE and Keeping of Your Brand

So, you've chosen a platform. You've set yourself up with a couple decent pics, your resume, all that. A potential employer or client can look you up and like what they see. Mission accomplished, right?

Well, it's good enough only if you're satisfied with the bare minimum. If you're looking to set yourself apart and ahead of other potential candidates, then it's up to you to keep working to improve your personal brand and increase your visibility. Being one of the results for John Doe and being *the* result for John Doe could really make the difference between getting the job and a better rate, and you will eventually find that the time spent on your digital image will be well worth it.

Your bare, base brand that you present should be that of an affable professional. If you're looking to stand out, though, then you need to think about the specifics of what you want to show others. What is it that you're looking to do or be an expert in? Create and display content that will present yourself as exactly *that*. Maybe you're already an expert in something, good on you. And how exactly are you going about advertising that?

Like most people, you're probably not doing any sort of self-promotion. How do you expect someone to know that you're the go-to for Cloud lift and shifts, or database upsizing, or Scrum Master-Master? You can't be in any way quiet or modest about your abilities here. If you want others to see your skills, you have to show them.

Luckily, this isn't that hard to do. You don't have to become a publicist just to get yourself out there. The easiest way to display your expertise is to keep a blog on the subject(s) of your expertise and regularly update it with relevant content.

It's not in any way embarrassing to admit that you may, perhaps, not know how to make and manage a website. If you don't have the time (or patience) to learn WordPress or some other CMS, then it's best to just go with a site-builder like Squarespace. They have a really user-friendly layout and you can probably get everything set up in under an hour.

Either way, you need to keep in mind that this is your brand and to ensure that you're clearly projecting that brand on the website. The picture you choose for yourself to put up on your website should be the same one for any and all of your other public profiles. Those that look you up might not recognize you, someone they may not have even yet met in person, across multiple pictures. They will, however, recognize the same picture that they've seen before. I also highly recommend that you include a contact page on your site, as publicly displaying your email all but guarantees that you'll receive a massive amount of spam.

Now as far as the actual blogging portion, what you need to write about is pretty obvious. What are you trying to get paid for? You want gigs doing what you know and what you specialize in, so that's what you need to write about. Remember, you're trying to build up trust in your abilities. When a prospective employer or client looks you up and finds your site, they need to feel like what they're seeing aligns with what it is that you do. So, make it align.

Anybody looking to potentially pay you for your knowledge in this area will see that not only do you really know your shit, you also know it enough to continue to educate yourself on what's new and changing in that subject area. That kind of evidence of your expertise *and* dedication to what makes you money is something that you just can't get across on a resume the way that you can here.

There's another route that you can go with this. Seeking out and engaging in digital debates or discussions on your area of expertise can also be a useful display of your knowledge. This is just as beneficial as keeping a blog, as having to defend and challenge points within your subject will show the depth of your knowledge. On top of that, the interaction with other people across these platforms will help raise your visibility, which of course will only aid in capturing the attention of a potential employer.

I personally recommend doubling up and doing both. Sure, it's time out of your day that doesn't directly get you paid, but it will ultimately prove to be an enormous help to secure the gigs (and rates) that you probably otherwise wouldn't. With either, though, it's important that you look over anything you're about to put online. It's pretty easy to make yourself look like an asshole on the Internet. It's also just as easy to prevent that by keeping a few things in mind before you make that post/comment/etcetera:

1.) Make sure that whatever you say is actually true. Fact-check yourself with a quick Google search or have decent evidence on hand to back up your claims.

2.) Staying civil is absolutely necessary, no matter the situation. Did you get in a friendly debate that turned into your challenger replying with personal attacks or obscenities? Doesn't matter. Keep your cool and cut the conversation. Firing back is only going to make you look bad, too.

3.) Review for spelling, grammar, typos, etc. You want to appear at least competent in the English language.

And as long as you refrain from any other obviously problematic public postings, your social media presence and engagement is going to give you that edge over other candidates. If you stay active and consistent with your postings, you'll get the algorithm on your side. The more you engage with platforms, the higher your name will appear in a Google search result. Review: activity makes your prominent, and prominence is *good*. Got it?

STAYING UP-TO-DATE

You're probably already aware that you can never get too comfy in this industry. We have to be sharks. If we quit swimming in the currents of technology, we'll die in the water. Keeping up with what's new doesn't even give you an edge. It's just necessary. None of us are allowed to rest on our knowledge for very long. If you want to have a hope of the next job, you need to know what's going on at all times.

It's hard to predict where things are going. You can't exactly forecast the future, especially with the recent uncertainties presented by the pandemic and current political environment. Luckily, at least, it's not too difficult to figure out what technology areas pays the best and/or has the most openings.

All you have to do here is hop on any site that lists jobs. LinkedIn, ZipRecruiter, Monster, Indeed, whatever. The beauty of these engines is that they collect and sort every available job, and you can specify your search however you'd like. But for this, you want to stay broad with the results. Type in very general titles like "web developer" and set your search range for the entire state. A title precise to what you're looking for or a city-wide result won't make for a decent sample size. Also, keep in mind that any previous searches or current information on your account may affect your search results. Algorithms will push gigs that you likely already know. If you find that your results are too specific, I recommend logging out and trying again. It may even be helpful to set your browser on private before searching, as to get results that are completely free from anything too tailored to you.

Check out their descriptions and requirements. Put aside about an hour to do this. Based on just this, it's going to be incredibly obvious what current technologies are in demand. If you don't know them, you better learn. If you already do, learn them better. Think of your skillset as a toolbox. You're not just some chump doing little home projects on the weekends. You're a master carpenter, and every saw and screw you have has to be continuously sharpened if you expect to stay in your trade.

I can't tell you what technology is hot at the precise time that you are reading this book. I can tell you, though, what was at the time of writing this book. I am typing this sentence in the middle of 2020, during the COVID-19 Pandemic, and here's what seems to be the predominant web skills right now: REACT, C#, Azure, Angular, and AWS. It's possible that these may still be in use by the time you read this, but it's just as possible that they've all fallen out of vogue in favor of something entirely new or different. The Internet, of course, is always updating. A quick look online will tell you what's what.

BEING the Prize

What a company ultimately looks for in a potential employee is someone who is going to add and create value within their workplace. Putting the time and effort in to present your brand and to stay up-to-date on the current technologies demonstrates that value well beyond what a resume could encompass, and will prove to be an investment that pays off immeasurably more than what you had put in.

Knowing that you are the prize, and acting like it, flips the script in the job search. You won't be grasping at any and all opportunities, grateful to even get an interview. You will have already gotten them to want you; it'll be in your power to pick where they want you the most. If you do this part exceptionally well, you can even push to see just how much any one company wants you in their employment.

You'll even get to put a number on it.

CHAPTER ELEVEN: CIRCUMVENTING THE ENTIRE SYSTEM

TLDR:

- Directly soliciting companies about their open positions could potentially let you bypass the technical recruiter.
- Direct solicitation does not always work, and companies may occasionally get exceptionally irritated over it.
- If they do, fuck them.

THE SYSTEM

Throughout this entire book, I've talked a lot about the system that we have in place. We, the IT tech people, spend years learning the various technologies and languages of computers. We, the ones with the actual knowledge and skills, look for the jobs that will pay us to implement what we've learned. There are more companies than I can count that desperately want to pay us to do what we can do. What we do is specialized and, unless some dystopian situation occurs and plunges us back into the pre-Internet ages, we will always be in demand.

This, then, should be an easy connection. Candidate to company, employee to employer. That's how it works in almost every other industry that I can think of. And yet, why is it that recruiters stand in the way?

The apparent idea is that they work as a conduit that would link the best person to the best job. Most of the time, though, the only thing that they may accomplish is throwing us into a misplaced position for an indecent rate. Most of the time, the only thing that they may accomplish is just fucking us over.

I've spent the last I-don't-even-know-how-many pages telling you how the system works and how to save yourself from getting fucked over by it. But there's something else. I can't, in good and clean conscience, not tell you about a better way altogether. Because yes, I really did find a better way.

I found a way around the entire system.

AROUND THE SYSTEM

I came to figure out how to bypass the dependence on recruiters quite some time ago—2004. I was at NASA at the time, working on a project for the United States Air Force and base operations. This project was coming toward an end, as all projects do, and I was starting to eye at the next gig. You know how that in-between is.

I got some through-the-grapevine info that Disney had a contract they were looking to fill. Seeing as I was looking to fill a new contract, you can probably put two and two together. All I needed was a recruiter to make the connection. Seems like a pretty easy-peasy situation, right?

Well, no. That apparently critical link between the contract and myself did not exist. I looked and asked around *everywhere*, but I failed to find a staffing company that could get me to the contract. I did, however, find out that the gig was going to be sourced internally and was *not* being advertised as of yet.

Most people would have just taken that fact for what it meant: Disney would find a good candidate from within, outsiders not considered. Most people would have just shrugged and then looked at what a recruiter was offering. But I, in all of the most annoying ways, am not like most people.

I've already said that I'm a bit of an asshole. I don't think I've mentioned that I'm also an obsessive. Like, once I decide that I want something, I really truly will not stop until I get it. I would rather work myself to death over something than admit defeat over *anything*. I'm a terrible loser and cannot take "no'" for an answer. It's obnoxious, I know. I try to reign it in most of the time, but it's come in handy on a few occasions. This is one of them.

So I set out like a dog on a bone and bit down on the supposedly impossible prospect. I made a couple calls and gathered just enough intel to figure out what area of Disney that the gig was at. I looked up all of the higher-ups for that area. And, yes, I possibly started to (lightly!) stalk any and all of the senior managers and directors that possibly had purview of this god damn gig. Remember, this was back in the days before LinkedIn. Getting that kind of information was tricky, to say the least.

I just needed an address. It took a couple days to get it. I searched and sleuthed until I had a physical address where these higher-ups could be contacted. And I came up with a (slightly!) dirty little idea about how to get their attention.

This is not an advertisement for FedEx. However, if you are going to do this, you should absolutely do it through FedEx.

The receiver never really knows what a FedEx package is about. Whatever you send, it's going to get opened. Especially if you're sending it to their office.

I cleaned up my resume and pitch letter, printed them out, and put it all together into a neat little package. I simultaneously FedExed my pitch and resume to the senior managers and an IT director. Then, I waited.

I understand that this tactic might come off as being too direct or dogged for some. That's fair; it *is* pretty direct and dogged. But the very nature of going over the recruiters' heads is already so against the fundamental system in place that *anything* you try here has the risk of coming off as too overt and therefore ineffective. If you're going to try to circumvent the system, you might as well try this. With this, you at least know that you'll catch their attention, however briefly that you might have it.

My package did get their attention. A couple days later, I even got an email from one of the senior managers. They gave me the name of one of the contracting companies that they were using for the job and invited me to apply. I applied through that company and got into an interview a week later. A little later after that, and I got that big call back. They were offering me the contract that'd been completely off-limits only a few weeks prior.

Now, I still had to deal with a recruiter. It seems like you can't completely avoid them in the course of getting hired, especially since I have never been interested in becoming an employee. However, this time our interactions were completely on my terms. They weren't the ones selling me off to the company. A senior manager had sent my info to the recruiter for the very job that they were looking to fill. Think about that for a minute: I was already wanted by the company, endorsed by a higher-up, and I knew it. However much you're imagining that helped during negotiations, you're probably right.

This wasn't just some one-off success, either. I later used this same exact method to nab my contracts at Hilton and with The Department of Defense. It's ballsy, sure, but a direct FedEx of your information is the single best way to get attention from the people that can get you in the door.

So, here's how you do it:

1.) Identify organizations that use your technology. This can be pretty easily accomplished by looking at an organization's current technology staff and the skills that they list out online. LinkedIn is perfect for this.

2.) Make a master document of information on each and all organizations that you research. I actually use the CRM HubSpot to track all this info.

3.) Under each individual organization, make a list of the senior managers and technology-related directors.

4.) Once you have this list more-or-less complete, now comes the hard part. How are you going to find an address that will receive a FedEx package and make its way to your intended target?

a.) Find where their office is listed. Find the local number associated with it. Call and ask: "What address can I send a package to in order for [intended recipient] to receive it?"

b.) If the person on the other end asks what the package is about, tell them that it is a personal matter. Specify that this is not something related to sales. If they don't find this response acceptable and keep pushing, then it's best just to admit that you are trying to send over your resume. Honesty won't necessarily kill your plan here, though. They'll still give you the address about half of the time. Otherwise, they can only otherwise tell you no.

c.) If you are absolutely desperate, you could always try to message someone in their technology department over LinkedIn for the address. You're likely to be surprised at how often this works.

5.) Once you've got that address down, you'll need to construct a *very* brief and concise paragraph that explains who you are and what it is that you want from them.

Example:

"Hello! My name is [your name] and I have been working with [whatever technology that you're looking to get hired for] for several years. As I understand, there is an opening within your organization for a web developer. Could you please tell me who I may speak with to possibly get an interview for this position? Thank you."

Anything along these lines is acceptable. It probably goes without saying, but make sure that you include your full name, your email, and your phone number.

6.) Send it. See what happens.

You can think of the standard hiring process like waiting in a line. That's what you're doing when you submit your resume to a job site or a recruiter. You're waiting in line, at the whim and mercy of whoever's in charge to pick your name out of a growing pile to move forward. I, personally, hate that shit.

By directly contacting the people who make the real decisions, you get to skip that line entirely. This mix of impatience and audacity can cause a little irritation in return, but I've found that this is easily pacified with good manners and some honesty.

I've done this to companies like Disney, Hilton, NASA, and a couple Fortune 500s in and around Florida. They were a little annoyed when they got back to me, but all is usually forgiven when I say this:

"I am sorry for being so direct, but I really believe that I am perfect for the position. This is my way of getting your attention."

Now, have any companies had a terminally negative reaction to my reaching out? Yes, of course. When you're going completely against the grain, it's bound to happen. And what does it matter if they do, anyway?

You do not have room in your life to worry about what people think, especially people that you'll never even meet. There are about 7.5ish billion people currently on the planet. The possibility of you running into *one* of them is just about nonexistent. Being embarrassed about your ill-received solicitation is not only a waste of time, but ultimately pointless.

I read somewhere that lions have a successful hunt only about 5% of the time. Even if you were playing with those odds, the chance to get to go over the recruiters' heads is more than worth it. And anyone that doesn't admire your chutzpah for daring to try taking the reins on your own destiny isn't worth knowing, let alone working for, anyways. As my now-dead father would say:

"Fuck 'em, as they aren't interesting enough to know."-Arthur Turman

AFTERWORD

The Grand Takeaway

If, for whatever odd reason, you've spent the money and time to read this and decide to only remember one thing, remember this: you can get *more*. You are worth *more*. But you will never get more if you don't ask for it.

Your game with recruiters needs to be calculated. Every move should be made to gather any and all evidence you can to strengthen your case in asking for a higher rate. You aren't here just for fun, after all. Go ahead and list out all of the pros that you can think of for working for any one company. Inevitably, the paycheck is going to close to or at the very top. Everybody wants to get paid, and everybody hopes to get paid well. You are not the one, idiotic exception.

What most candidates fail to consider is that the person they're speaking to really does want to fill this position, whatever their true reasons may be. You have to give them every reason possible to pick you, but you also can't shy away from asking for what you want and need in return.

Money is not the only thing that you can ask for, either.

Any good negotiator will try to maximize any and all benefits that they can possibly gain. If they won't agree to an increase in the rate, there are still some other valuables left on the table: more vacation, lower insurance, flexible time off, etc. There is always, always *something*. It's up to you to figure out what it is and ask for it.

The Rulebook

You can think of this book as an instruction manual for playing the game. If you follow what I've told you, my hope is that you can at least get more out of a gig than you would have without reading this. An entire book is obviously going to be difficult to recall, of course.

So I've devised an abbreviated master list of everything the book has covered. This is going to be your rulebook. If you're going to toss this book now that you're done, I urge you to at the very least tear this page out. Fold it up in your wallet or stick it on your mirror. This is everything you absolutely need to know.

Good luck out there.

TURMAN'S RULES OF ENGAGEMENT

For Dealing with Recruiters

#1: Only divulge information that benefits you.

#2: Always be polite, as nobody wants to work with an asshole.

#3: Figure out who it is that you're talking to before you tell them anything.

#4: Know your quantitative worth.

#5: What you were paid in the past is none of their business. If they ask, do not answer.

#6: Never tell a recruiter that you need the job right now.

#7: Never tell a recruiter where else you are interviewing at.

#8: Never tell a recruiter how much you want the job.

#9: Never tell a recruiter about any future plans that could flag you as a shorter-term employee than the company is looking for.

#10: Do what you can to not have to make the first offer. Postpone salary discussions as far into the process as possible.

#11: If you are forced to make the first offer, then give a

range with your most acceptable number at the low end. Don't throw out some outrageous number, as it will only backfire.

#12: Get all the facts of the job (commute, benefits, etc.) before you make your counter-offer.

#13: Ask a consistent set of questions for every job that you consider. Note down the answers and use them for comparison between positions, and to ultimately make an educated choice among them.

#14: Use the facts of the job (commute, benefits, etc.) as a basis to negotiate for a higher salary.

#15: Negotiate farther, even if the numbers go beyond your wildest imagination.

#16: You are the prize. Act like it.

FURTHER READING

Voss, Chris. *Never Split the Difference: Negotiating As If Your Life Depended On It.* Harper Business, 2016.

Thompson, Leigh. "Negotiation Tips: Who's on first?" Northwestern Kellogg.

ACKNOWLEDGMENTS

Thanks again to all of the recruiters, good and bad both, for creating the unfortunate need to write this book. Thank you to Zoe Rose for helping me finish this god damn book that I've been trying to write for the past five years. Thank you to Scott Johnson for becoming my reluctant mentor and nudging me toward a CS career. And thank you to every associate, recruiter, employer, and others that I met along the way and ended up in this book as advice, anecdotes, or horror stories. Thank you.

ABOUT THE AUTHOR

Scott Turman

Scott Turman has developed software and cryptographic systems for organizations such as NASA, Disney, Hilton, the Florida House of Representatives, and the Department of Defense. He's conducted hundreds of technical interviews throughout his career and has interacted with about as many recruiters. Scott has not had to deal with a recruiter in over eight years, and now uses his experience in the industry to teach others. He lives with his wife and son in Maitland, Florida.

If you would like more information on Scott's next books, projects, or products, please visit his website below.

https://www.scottturman.com

Zoe Rose

Zoe Rose received a B.F.A. in English from FSU in 2020. Her fiction work has appeared in *Eyrie Art and Literary* and *The Kudzu Review*, among others. She lives in Orlando. You can find more information on her past and current projects at the website below.

https://www.zoeirose.com